Puppy Training for Kids

by Colleen Pelar

Photos by Amber Johnson

BARRON'S

Dedication

To children and puppies,
who spread love, laughter, and fun wherever they go.

About the Author

In addition to *Puppy Training for Kids*, Colleen Pelar has written two books for adults: *Living with Kids and Dogs . . . Without Losing Your Mind* and *Kids and Dogs: A Professional's Guide to Helping Families*. Her company, Dream Dog Productions, specializes in teaching people about how dogs communicate. Colleen speaks on dog-related topics at seminars all over the United States and Canada.

Colleen has been crazy about dogs since she was a little girl. She's had canine best friends her whole life. But just living with dogs wasn't enough; Colleen always wanted to learn more about them and to help other people appreciate dogs, too. That led her to become a dog trainer, which she thinks is the best job in the world.

Photos © Amber Johnson/Modern Life Photo
www.modernlifephoto.com

© Copyright 2012 by Barron's Educational Series, Inc.

All inquiries should be addressed to:
Barron's Educational Series, Inc.
250 Wireless Boulevard
Hauppauge, New York 11788
www.barronseduc.com

ISBN: 978-1-4380-0099-2

All information and advice contained in this book has been reviewed by a veterinarian.

Library of Congress Catalog Card No.: 2011046395

Library of Congress Cataloging-in-Publication
Pelar, Colleen
   Puppy training for kids / by Colleen Pelar
      p. cm.
   Includes index.
   ISBN 978-1-4380-0099-2
   1. Puppies—Training. I. Title.
SF431.P427 2012
636.7'0887—dc23   2011046395

Date of manufacture: September 2017
Manufactured by: V05I05N, Dongguan City, China
19 18 17 16 15 14 13 12 11

A Word About Pronouns

Many dog lovers feel that the pronoun "it" is not appropriate when referring to a pet that can be such a wonderful part of our lives. For this reason, dogs are described as "she" throughout this book unless the topic specifically relates to male dogs. No gender bias is intended by this writing style.

A Note for Parents

This book has been written to foster a healthy, safe, and loving relationship between your child and a new puppy.

The benefits of growing up with a dog are numerous. Children learn about compassion, kindness, and responsibility, and they gain companionship and lots of fun in return.

All of the activities in this book are designed to be fun and safe for both the child and the puppy. However, an adult should always supervise when children are interacting with dogs. For this reason, we recommend that you and your child read this book together and that you carefully monitor all the care and training your child provides for your puppy.

If you have any concerns about your puppy's behavior, especially toward children, please contact your veterinarian for a referral to a behavior specialist. Don't wait, hoping the puppy will grow out of the behavior. Early intervention is important.

CONTENTS

Introduction To Puppy Training

Dogs make wonderful friends. They love spending time with you. They're terrific listeners, and they never tell your secrets.

Dogs know what is really important. Your puppy won't care if you are popular, smart, athletic, or funny. She only wants you to be a kind friend whom she can love, trust, and rely on. Friendship is a two-way street. By learning more about dogs, you can create that special bond with your puppy.

It's not all fun and games, though. Having a dog in the family is both a responsibility and a privilege. There's a lot of work involved. Sometimes kids want a dog more than their parents do. The parents say, "Dogs are too much work. We don't have time for a dog." The dog-loving kids promise that they'll help with everything. They'll walk

PARENT BOX:

The Best Dogs for Kids

Always choose a puppy based on behavior, not breed. Don't be fooled by articles that say specific breeds are kid-friendly. Some of those dogs will love kids. Some won't. You can't choose a good dog by breed alone.

Within every litter, there can be a wide range of behavior. Just as you aren't exactly like your siblings, your puppy isn't exactly like hers, either.

Go into your search with an open mind. Pay attention to each puppy's personality. It's easy to be swayed by appearances, but the really important characteristics are on the inside.

You want a dog that's sweet and social, not skittish or shy. The best dogs are easy-going and bounce back well from slightly stressful situations. They enjoy hanging out with people and handle change well.

These special dogs come in every shape, size, and appearance. There's a wonderful puppy waiting for you, but she may not look quite like you expected.

Puppy Jobs—Friday

ACTIVITY	NAME	DONE?
Morning walk	Dad	✓
Breakfast	Kayla	✓
Training	Mom and James	✓
Afternoon walk	Mom, James, and Kayla	✓
Scoop the yard	Kayla	✓
Dinner	James	✓
Stuff chew toys	Kayla	✓
Vacuum	James	✓

the dog, feed her, brush her, and even scoop the poop! If you made a promise like that, be sure to keep it.

Many families create a responsibility chart, like the one above, so that everyone can take part. Be sure to rotate jobs so that everyone participates. If you have younger siblings, find jobs they can help with too, such as scooping dog food into the bowl.

Here's a chart for you to use. Fill in the name of each person who will be completing the activity listed. Then check off each one when it has been completed.

Puppy Jobs—

(Insert Day of Week Here)

ACTIVITY	NAME	DONE?
Morning walk		
Breakfast		
Training		
Afternoon walk		
Scoop the yard		
Dinner		
Stuff chew toys		
Vacuum		

GETTING OFF TO A GOOD START

Puppies are learning all the time—not just when we think we're teaching them—so you need to be aware of how your behavior affects your puppy's behavior.

For example, if you drop your napkin on the floor and your puppy picks it up, what you do today may change what she does next time. If you chase her, grab her, and wrestle the napkin from her mouth, she'll learn to be very quick and to hide when she has something she wants. On the other hand, if you call her over to you using a happy voice and trade a tasty treat for the napkin, she'll learn to bring things to you when she finds something interesting. Then you can decide whether it is something she'll be allowed to keep.

I Told You Not to Do That!

Even when they know the rules, sometimes kids don't follow them completely. Your job is to model good interactions with dogs and also to coach your kids to help them improve their dog skills. As with all coaching, this takes time, consistency, and a fair amount of repetition before the message really sticks. Be patient.

In both cases, the puppy is doing what seems to work best in that situation. Consequences—what happens next—are one of the best ways of telling whether your puppy will do the same thing again. If a friend pets your puppy when she jumps up, your puppy will jump on other people when she wants attention. Keep this in mind. You may need to remind your friends that your puppy shouldn't be allowed to do things that you don't want her to do when she's full grown.

Be a Good Teacher

What are your goals for your puppy? What would you like your dog to be able to do with you and your family? Make a list. This will help you and your parents stay on track with training.

Just as your teachers help you learn new things, you are one of your puppy's teachers. You need to help her learn how to be safe and well behaved. The best way to do this is to reward her often when she's doing well. When she's rewarded for good behavior, she'll keep doing it and soon it will become a habit. Your puppy will be good at being good.

Help her by not letting her make any big mistakes. Put away things she shouldn't have. Watch her carefully so that you can distract her with one of her toys when she sees something she shouldn't have. Let your puppy know when she is doing things right, and step in quickly to prevent poor choices.

PUPPY SUPPLIES

Shopping for puppy supplies is fun. There are so many different things that your puppy may enjoy. Buying supplies can be overwhelming—and expensive.

Be sure that the things you buy are right for your puppy. Some things may be better for older dogs or for dogs that are smaller or larger than yours. Read the labels carefully.

Food and Treats

Many veterinarians and trainers believe that eating right can help prevent health and behavior problems. Since your puppy will eat the same food most days, it's very important to make healthy choices.

Read all of the ingredients on the label when selecting food. The most healthful dog foods avoid dyes, artificial preservatives,

> ### Food is a Great Teaching Tool—Don't Waste It
> Don't always feed your puppy in her bowl. Have her work for it instead! Scoop her meal into a treat bag and use it to train her. You can also create fun games, such as hunting for kibble tossed in the yard. Having her work for her food teaches her to focus on you.

by-products, and fillers. These are listed under the ingredients on the food label. Some examples are butylated hydroxyanisole (BHA), butylated hydroxytoluene (BHT), and FD&C red dye #40.

Choose healthy treats for training, too. Chicken, liver, beef, cheese, and salmon are delicious and nutritious treats for dogs.

Bowls

Choose bowls that are easy to carry. You'll want to rinse the food and water bowls out each time before you fill them. Look for a bowl with a stable base so it won't tip and spill.

as a correction. These kinds of collars can make a dog feel nervous and panicky.

Identification

Your puppy needs an ID tag with her name and your contact information. An ID tag will help her find her way home if she ever gets loose. It's a vital piccc of safety equipment.

Many families also get a microchip ID for their puppies. A microchip is embedded under the skin by a veterinarian and can be read by a special scanner. When a lost dog goes to an animal shelter and does not have an ID tag, the staff will scan the dog to look for a microchip.

Leash

Buy a leather or nylon 4–6-foot (1.2–1.8 m) leash for walks and training.

If your puppy is going to be big and strong when she's full grown, get a leather leash. It will be more comfortable in your hands.

Extension leashes are not recommended, because they teach your puppy to pull. These leashes consist of a  handle with a long cord coiled inside that extends and retracts when the dog pulls (shown above).

Crate

Choose a crate that's just big enough for your puppy to stand up, turn around, and lie back down. If your puppy has too much room, she may use one end of the crate for potty breaks. This would make it much harder for her to learn to go to the bathroom only in her potty area outdoors.

Collar

Get a basic nylon collar for your puppy. The collar should fit comfortably, and you should be able to get a few fingers between the collar and your dog's neck. Be sure that the collar isn't too loose. You don't want it to slip off.

When you first put her collar on, your puppy may sit down and try to scratch it off. The collar isn't hurting her, but it's a new and different feeling for her. It's very distracting at first. Soon she won't even notice it.

Avoid using metal collars or any kind of collar that tightens around your dog's neck

Harness

There are different kinds of dog harnesses. Some make dogs better at pulling; others make it easier for you to walk a strong dog. Be sure to choose a harness that helps you.

Harnesses that connect in the back, like sled dogs wear, give a dog more pulling power. You may find it difficult to walk your puppy if she wears this kind of harness.

Harnesses that connect to the leash on the front of the dog's chest help teach better leash manners.

With a harness that connects in the front, your puppy will pull less. This makes it easier for a person to walk a dog—especially a bouncy, silly dog—because you don't have to be as strong.

Toys

Buy a few rubber toys that you can stuff with food and treats. These are great ways for you to give your puppy something appropriate to chew. (See "How to Keep Your Puppy Out of Trouble" for tips for stuffing these toys.) Check the tag to be sure the toy is the right size for your puppy. A toy that is too small could hurt her tongue.

Most puppies enjoy squeaky toys, too. Be sure to get ones that can't be easily torn by sharp teeth. Throw away any damaged toys to be sure that your puppy doesn't eat anything she shouldn't.

YOUR PUPPY'S FIRST YEAR

Birth to 8 Weeks

Puppies are born helpless—but they don't stay that way for long!

Newborn puppies are blind, deaf, and toothless, but their noses work well. Their mother will stay close by to take care of them. The puppies can locate her by smell and touch. When they are about 2 weeks old, their eyes and ear canals open, and puppies begin walking at about 3 weeks.

By 4 weeks old, puppies are beginning to explore. Their very sharp puppy teeth are coming in, and they start to eat solid food. Learning to be gentle with her teeth is a lesson in manners that your puppy learns between 4

and 8 weeks. If she nips her mother or siblings too hard, they will move away from her.

She needs practice to learn how to use her mouth in a way that doesn't hurt

Wait Until She's Ready

Don't get a puppy before she turns 8 weeks old. She needs every moment of that time to learn from her mother and littermates.

Start preparing for your puppy while you wait for her to come home. Set up safe areas for her to sleep, eat, and play.

anyone. Most puppies learn this lesson well with other dogs. Then when they join their new human family, they need additional practice. Our skin is more delicate, so bites that didn't hurt your puppy's siblings may still make you jump!

The first two months are a very important time for a puppy. If a puppy is separated from her mother during this time and/or if she doesn't have any siblings, she may have trouble getting along with other dogs when she's an adult. She won't understand their signals if she misses out on learning these doggy social skills—ones that people can't fully teach her.

8 Weeks to 4 Months

Most puppies are between 8 and 16 weeks old when they come home. This period is called the socialization

window; it is the best time to teach puppies about the world. Chapter 2 is full of ideas to help your puppy grow up confident and happy.

Everything in your home will be new to your puppy. Make sure that you've put away anything that could hurt her. She won't know what's safe and what's not. She'll probably sniff and then try to bite almost everything— even things like doorstops, corners of walls, and the straps on your backpack. Puppies aren't choosy. If she doesn't know what something is, she'll probably taste it. Human babies like to put things in their mouths, too. It's a way of exploring the world.

Puppies Are Not Dolls

Please don't carry your puppy around. She may be adorable, but she's not a toy. Being held and carried can make your puppy nervous. She may wiggle and squirm to try to get down, which isn't safe.

When you want your puppy to be with you, call her name. If you find your puppy doesn't come, practice, practice, practice! Don't just grab her and carry her.

Crates

A crate is the best place to leave your puppy when you can't watch her. When she's in her crate, she won't chew an electrical cord, pull the pillows off the couch, or have an accident on the carpet. Keep in mind, though, that a crate doesn't teach your puppy what she should do. It just helps keep her safe.

Whenever possible, have your puppy with you so that you can teach her how to behave in every situation.

Petting Puppies

Welcome Petting	Uncomfortable Petting
Gentle, slow strokes	Rapid pat-pat-patting
Touching without holding on or grabbing	Holding on, squeezing, or hugging
Being careful around her sensitive eyes and ears	Patting on top of her head
Encouraging a puppy to come toward you	Grabbing her collar and pulling her toward you

fingers! If you can't be right beside her, put her in her crate for a rest.

During this period, your puppy will be learning a lot about people. Just as your baby brother or sister needs to learn to be gentle with his or her hands, your puppy needs to learn to be careful with her teeth. If she nips you, it may sting a little, but her puppy teeth can't do much damage.

To help her learn to use her mouth more gently, always keep

Stay with her when she's exploring. When she goes toward something she shouldn't have, distract her with a better choice. Give her a chew toy when she wants to nibble on a chair leg, or your a toy handy. When she uses her teeth on anything—or anyone—she shouldn't, offer her the toy instead.

If she nips you, give a quick yelp and then freeze for a moment. This is the same signal her mother and siblings used. Your puppy will probably stop and look surprised. Quickly give her the toy to chew on. If she doesn't take the toy and instead nips at you again, she clearly needs a break. Put her in her crate with her toy for a few minutes to give her time to settle down and unwind. (Depending on how excited she's gotten, it may be better for a parent to put her in the crate for this break.)

She needs to learn that if she hurts you, you stop playing. In any play session, it's nice to give her two chances. The first time she's too rough, yelp to let her know that it hurts, and then offer her a toy. If it happens a second time, she'll lose her playmate for a while. After all, good friends try not to hurt each other.

Be calm and quiet when you are teaching her to be gentle. Jumping, yanking your hand away, or shrieking will rev your puppy up, not calm her down. Have patience. She doesn't realize yet that it hurts you.

Even at 8 weeks old, your puppy is ready to learn, so start training her right away. She will learn quickly. Keep a careful watch to be sure she doesn't get into anything she shouldn't. Careful supervision and puppy proofing help keep your puppy safe, but they also prevent your puppy

---

PARENT BOX:

An Ounce of Prevention

When we think of a child being bitten by a dog, the common image is of a loose, unfamiliar dog running toward a child on a playground. This rarely happens. In the vast majority of dog-bite cases, the dog and the child know each other. The most common scenario is a bite from the family dog, but bites also occur at relatives', friends', and neighbors' homes.

Don't think that just because your child is often around a specific dog that the two of them communicate well. Learn about canine body language so you'll know what to look for and when to intervene. (See the "Canine Communication" chapter for more information.) If you have any concerns about the interactions between your child and a dog, separate them immediately and contact a trainer for help with improving their relationship.

Hmm, What Do I Smell?

People tend to notice how things look, but dogs pay more attention to how they smell. Your puppy's nose is 1,000 times more powerful than yours. She can identify very specific things by odor alone. When dogs greet, they can tell each other's age, sex, and health with just a quick sniff.

When meeting one of your friends, your puppy will not only notice what he looks like, but she'll also be able to tell that he had syrup at breakfast, used a pencil at school, and has a cell phone in his pocket. It's easy for her.

The scents are each distinct and identifiable.

Your puppy will remember people better by what they smell like than by what they look like.

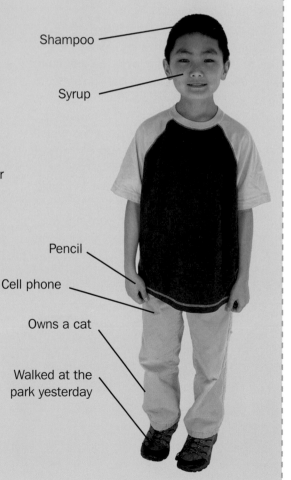

Shampoo

Syrup

Pencil

Cell phone

Owns a cat

Walked at the park yesterday

from discovering the joy of shredding news-papers. It's your job to keep her out of trouble.

5 months to 9 months

By 5 months old, your puppy can almost be considered a teenager. She'll be much more comfortable and confident in your home.

This confidence may mean she won't always listen as well as she used to. Some-times she may not come when you call her. She'll look up from what she's doing, glance over at you, and then look away. She doesn't want to end her fun. That's a normal part of growing up. Don't get discouraged. Keep training and keep rewarding her for all the good choices she makes. This is just a

Dog Years

It's fun to compare your puppy's age with your own. People often say that each calendar year equals seven years for a dog. It's not quite that simple. The first two years of a dog's life have the greatest amount of change and devel-opment, so they count for more than seven years each.

By age 1, your puppy is about 16, and at age 2, your puppy could be con-sidered a 24-year-old. But the next few years don't add up as quickly. Generally you can add five years for each year after the second. So a 6-year-old dog would be 44 (24 + 5 + 5 + 5 + 5 = 44).

This isn't an exact calculation, of course. Very large dogs tend to age more quickly. Irish Wolfhounds usually live only six to eight years. Small dogs tend to live the longest. The average life span of dogs is about 12-1/2 years.

phase, and your strong relationship will win in the end.

By this stage, your puppy will have several adult teeth and may be getting her molars. She'll need to chew a lot! Losing her puppy teeth and getting adult ones can be very uncomfortable. Chewing helps to ease the pain. Keep her well supplied with chew toys. Try freezing them so they'll be more soothing. Be ready to offer a chew toy any time she considers chewing something she shouldn't.

Now that she's a bit older, she's ready for more exercise too. How much she needs depends on her breed characteris-tics, but puppies between 5 and 9 months definitely need more exercise than they did at 4 months.

In fact, you may start to see "the puppy crazies" from time to time. Sometimes a puppy will get very excited and run around

Most Popular Breeds

In a recent survey, the 20 most popular breeds in the United States were as follows:

1. Labrador Retrievers
2. German Shepherd Dogs
3. Yorkshire Terriers
4. Beagles
5. Golden Retrievers
6. Bulldogs
7. Boxers
8. Dachshunds
9. Poodles
10. Shih Tzu
11. Rottweilers
12. Miniature Schnauzers
13. Chihuahuas
14. Doberman Pinschers
15. Pomeranians
16. German Shorthaired Pointers
17. Great Danes
18. Siberian Huskies
19. Shetland Sheepdogs
20. Boston Terriers

Everybody Makes Mistakes

Mistakes are an important part of learning, but the best teachers help students succeed. Help your puppy make good choices by supervising her very carefully. Always look around to make sure there isn't anything dangerous that she could get into.

If you notice her sniffing the floor, immediately take her out for a potty break. When she tries to chew something that she shouldn't, give her one of her toys to chew on instead.

When you can't watch her, put your puppy in her crate. But remember that a crate doesn't teach her anything; it only keeps her safe. She needs your help to learn how she should behave in your home and neighborhood.

the house at top speed. She'll run until she's tired, and then she'll flop down for a rest. Some parents think the puppy crazies are funny; others don't like this kind of activity in the house. If your parents don't like it, be sure that your puppy gets lots of exercise outside each day so that she'll be able to resist if she's hit by a sudden urge to race around.

Many "problem behaviors," such as digging, barking, chewing, and jumping, develop between 5 and 9 months. Giving your puppy lots of supervised, appropriate, and aerobic exercise will help. After all, those problem behaviors are really just things that bored dogs like to do.

10 to 12 months

It's tempting to think that your puppy is an adult by the time she reaches 10 to 12 months old. She has all of her adult teeth, she's probably almost as tall as she's going to be, and she's usually good around the house. But she's not all grown up yet!

This is a great time to work on good manners in public. She's probably learned *sit*, *down*, and *stay* in the living room, but will she do them in the pet store or at the park? Take treats and practice basic skills with her wherever you go.

The real world is far more distracting than your house. You'll probably have to make things a little easier to help her succeed. Find quiet areas to work with your puppy. Don't put her in the middle of the action. Remember that when you reward a behavior, you make it stronger, so pay careful attention to everything she's doing right.

At home, let your puppy earn privileges slowly. When she hasn't had any housetraining accidents for two months and chews only her toys, start by leaving her unsupervised for just a minute as you go get something from another room. (This is usually after she's lived with you for several months. If you adopt an older puppy, be sure she's had time to fully adjust to your home before you try this.)

When she does well with that, you can try leaving her for longer periods. Build up gradually. Ask someone to check on the puppy while you take a shower or do some homework.

If she's comfortable being left alone for 15–30 minutes, try actually leaving the house. Give her only one room to be in. Use a baby gate or close the door to make sure she doesn't leave the area you've puppy proofed.

Remember, you are making decisions for your puppy. It's not fair to be angry with her if she gets into something when you made the decision to leave her loose. If you aren't prepared to take responsibility for what she does, then be sure to put her in her crate when you can't keep an eye on her.

GROOMING

Your puppy doesn't need to bathe as often as you do, but she does need regular grooming to keep her body healthy and strong. Her skin produces oils that help keep her coat clean—and also make it water resistant!

Regular brushing will stimulate your puppy's hair follicles and remove dirt from her coat. In addition, frequent grooming helps you spot issues, such as ticks, broken nails, or hot spots, before they become big problems. And finally, puppies who are groomed regularly and learn to enjoy it are much easier to handle when they are full grown.

Your puppy will be so interested in exploring that she may not want to stay still for a full brushing at first. That's okay. Start by doing lots of short, fun sessions so that your puppy will learn to enjoy being groomed. You might brush her left side one time and her right the next.

To help keep her still and happy, you could ask someone to stand in front of her and give her treats. She'll be more focused on your helper and the delicious treats than on what you are doing. (Remind your helper not to move around or else your puppy will be moving around too.)

You can also get permission from a parent to put a glob of peanut butter on a stationary item nearby to give her something to focus on. Brush her while she licks it off. Be sure to clean up afterward!

Don't sneak up on your puppy. Give her a moment to sniff the brush before you begin. As she learns to enjoy grooming sessions, she'll be excited to see the brush whenever you bring it out.

Be very gentle and use long, slow strokes. Brush in the direction her fur grows. If you find a mat or knot, look it over before trying to detangle it. Can you gently rub it out with your fingers or by using a wide-toothed comb? For some mats, you may need an adult's help.

18

Let's Take a Bath!

Some dogs are afraid of getting a bath, so be sure to make it fun for your puppy. She may be very wiggly. Use treats to distract her and work quickly so that she'll be out of the tub and running around again as soon as possible.

Bathing a dog is usually a two-person job so ask your parent to help you. Be prepared to get wet! Get organized before you start your puppy's bath so that you can easily reach everything you need.

Use a bucket or shower attachment with warm water to get your puppy completely wet before putting shampoo on. Her coat may be surprisingly water resistant from those protective oils. Be very careful with shampoo and water around her face. You may want to use a wet washcloth for her face rather than pouring water on her head.

Work the shampoo through her coat and then rinse her very well. Go over her body a few times with warm-water rinses to be sure you get all of the shampoo out. If you miss a spot, it could make her itchy and uncomfortable.

When she's clean, wrap her in a towel and gently dry her off as much as possible. When you are done towel-drying her, she'll likely roll around to try to dry herself more. If you are inside, she'll be rolling on the carpet, but outside, she may roll in dirt before you can catch her. Then you'll have to bathe her all over again! Keep your puppy somewhere warm until she's fully dry so she won't be uncomfortably chilled.

PARENT BOX:

Grooming Jobs for Grownups

Kids can do a great job of bathing and brushing dogs, but some jobs, such as ear cleaning, nail trimming, and tooth brushing, are better left to adults.

All of these activities require some level of restraint and can make your puppy feel trapped or uncomfortable. With gentle handling and patience, you can teach your puppy that these activities are nothing to worry about.

Visiting the Veterinarian

Puppies visit the doctor many times in their first year. Your puppy's veterinarian will track her growth and development. Your puppy will also get several immunization shots to prevent particular diseases.

Many adult dogs are afraid of their veterinarian's office. This is usually because something painful or scary happened there. They may be afraid of the high examination table, the slippery floors, or having strangers touch them. Since the dogs don't understand what's happening, a visit to the veterinarian can be very scary for them.

Imagine that you hurt your shoulder and had to go to the hospital. In addition to taking X-rays, a doctor might want to feel your shoulder and see how well it moves. This might hurt, but the doctor would explain everything before touching you so you would know what to expect. Understanding what's happening can make a doctor's visit less scary.

When your puppy goes to the animal hospital, she doesn't know that the veterinarian is there to help her. Since she doesn't understand your words, you can't explain. However, you can help your puppy feel safer and more comfortable at the veterinarian's office by making her puppy checkups as stress-free as possible. Here's how:

- Visit the waiting room even when you don't have an appointment. Spend two or three minutes in the lobby. Give your puppy a chance to go in, sit down, have a few treats, say hello to the office staff, and then leave. This will teach her that going to the veterinarian can be fun.

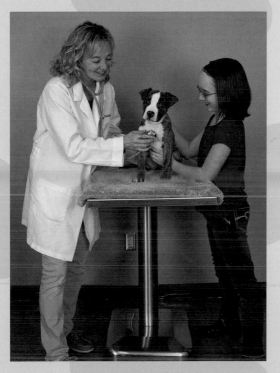

- Take treats when you go for your appointment. Practice some of your puppy's new skills to keep her mind occupied.
- Try not to overwhelm your puppy. Too many people talking to her or touching her can be stressful rather than supportive. (The waiting room is also not a good place for you to meet other dogs because they may be nervous or worried.)
- If you are asked to keep her still for any part of the exam, be sure to hold her snugly so she feels secure, but not so tightly that she feels squashed.

The more fun your puppy has at the veterinarian's office, the less worried she'll be about going. All dogs need regular checkups throughout their lives, so spend some time now to make your puppy feel safe and happy at the doctor's office.

Housetraining Your Puppy

Puppies have to learn that they shouldn't wet the carpet. You'll need to teach your puppy where to go to the bathroom. At first, this job is more about how well you do than how well your puppy does.

Until they are 3 to 4 months old, puppies don't have very good control of their bladders. When they realize they need to go, they're going to need to go very soon. You'll need to watch your puppy carefully so that you can take her out fast.

Changing Activities

Your puppy may be able to go three or four hours without a bathroom break when she's sleeping, but when she's awake, she'll need to go more often.

Plan to take your puppy out at least once every hour when she's awake, but don't be surprised if she needs to go out even more often.

The best guideline is to take your puppy out for a potty break every time there's a change of activity. When she wakes up, take her out. After she eats, take her out. After she drinks, take her out. When she finishes playing, take her out.

You get the idea. Take her out often!

Your puppy's favorite potty spot will soon become wherever she goes to the bathroom most often, so be careful. You don't want her favorite spot to be the living room carpet!

PICKING A POTTY SPOT

To begin, choose an area to use as the potty spot. Pick a spot that is easy to get to because you'll need to hurry, at least at first. Talk to your parents to find out where the potty area should be.

You'll take your puppy to her potty spot many times a day. Hurry to the chosen spot. Don't let your puppy sniff along the way. Once you get to the potty spot, you can let your puppy sniff around. Be calm and quiet while you wait for her.

Soon she'll slow down and sniff the ground. That's a sign that she's nearly ready to go potty. After she goes, praise her and give her a treat right away. Now that she's empty, you can begin to play with her. By not playing until after she goes to the bathroom, you'll teach her to go out and take care of her business quickly so that the fun can begin again.

What If My Puppy Doesn't Go?

If you wait for several minutes in the potty area and she does not go to the bathroom, take her back in. Watch her very carefully for signs that she may need to relieve herself. If you see any, rush her back out to the potty spot. Soon you'll have success.

If you can't keep a close eye on her, put her back in her crate. When you are ready to bring your puppy out of the crate, go to the potty spot first. Be sure not to play with her, but watch her carefully. Praise and reward her when she goes.

By taking her out often and rewarding her with treats and attention every time she uses her potty spot, you'll quickly teach your puppy how to stay clean in the house. Every family wants their dog to earn an A I in housetraining.

ACCIDENTS

Don't get angry if your puppy has an accident in the house. It's not her fault. She's still learning.

Treat Timing

Some people stand in the doorway and watch their puppy in the yard. Then they'll give her a treat when she comes in. The puppy thinks the treat is for coming back in the house, not for relieving herself in the proper area.

Go out with your puppy—even if it's cold or wet out (maybe even especially if it's cold or wet out). Reward her as soon as she goes in the potty spot, because you want her to know that she did the right thing.

23

The basics of housetraining are simple. The real challenge is watching your puppy so closely that you catch her before she has an accident. The better you supervise, the more quickly she'll learn.

Let's Stick Together

Most housetraining accidents happen when people aren't watching the puppy carefully. Supervising is more than just being nearby. To supervise a puppy, you need to be watching her carefully, paying attention to what she is doing, and being ready to intervene in a split second.

You may want to wear your puppy's leash around your waist like a belt so that she'll always be close by. Use an easy-to-open clip, like a carabiner, to secure it. This way your puppy will never be more than 4 feet (1.2 m) from you.

The better the supervision a puppy has, the quicker she'll learn to use her designated potty spot.

How Clean Is Clean?

Do a good job when you clean up any puppy accidents. Be sure that the area not only looks clean, but also really is clean.

When You Gotta Go, You Gotta Go

Puppies often don't give you much warning before they wet the floor (especially in the first few weeks). It takes a while for them to learn to give you a signal that they'd like to go out.

Be patient, and be observant. The most common signals are the puppy slowing down, circling, and sniffing the ground more intently. Often her tail will change position, too. If you see one of those signs indoors, rush your puppy to the potty area.

Housetraining takes time. As your puppy gets older, she'll be able to wait a little longer between potty breaks.

If you seem angry, she could be frightened. Since she won't understand why you are upset, she may think that you don't like her to go to the bathroom at all. She needs to relieve herself (everyone does!), so she could start to hide from you to do it. That's a much bigger problem than cleaning up one accident.

Scooping

Scooping isn't fun, but it needs to be done. Always carry bags with you when you walk your puppy so you can clean up after her.

You'll also need to tend to the potty area in your yard from time to time. No one likes a dirty bathroom. If there isn't enough clear space, your puppy may choose to relieve herself somewhere else. You definitely don't want that.

Five minutes of scooping now and then will keep the task manageable and the yard clean.

Remember that the scent of urine can be a trigger for puppies to go in that spot again. Use products made to get rid of pet odors, not just ones that make things smell good to people. Ask an adult to help you clean the mess properly.

Be Patient

It will take a while before your puppy is fully housetrained. Be patient. If you don't notice your puppy's signals, she might have an accident in the house. She'll do best if you take her out often. Always take her out as soon as she wakes up, but also be sure to take her out any time you've been playing for a while and shortly after each meal.

It's really important to pay close attention so that your puppy does not have accidents in the house. Otherwise, she may not learn that you want her to use *only* the outdoor potty area. If she's having trouble, try these tips:

- Watch her more closely to learn her early-warning signals.
- Reward her with treats and praise when she goes potty outside.
- Thoroughly clean up any accidents—ask an adult for help if needed.
- Put her in her crate when you can't supervise her.

CRATE TRAINING

Dogs like dens, which are cozy, private areas for resting. Your puppy's crate will give her security and also help with housetraining.

Crates are a safe place for puppies to sleep and stay clean. Dogs and puppies prefer to go to the bathroom away from their sleeping areas. For this reason, a crate encourages your puppy to learn to hold her bladder. Healthy puppies in properly sized crates rarely go to the bathroom in them. When they do, it may be a sign that they aren't feeling well, or that they didn't live in a clean environment in their first few weeks of life. If you know that your puppy was born in a clean environment and you notice that she is going to the bathroom in her crate often, speak to a parent about taking your puppy to the veterinarian for a check-up to make sure she is healthy.

When choosing a place for your puppy's crate, it's best to be close to a door so you can quickly and easily get her outside for potty breaks. Make sure this is also a safe, quiet spot so your puppy can get plenty of rest.

Use the crate at bedtime, but also during the day when you can't supervise her. It's important for her to learn to feel safe and happy by herself when people are around but not available to play with her.

Click for Good Behavior

Clickers are little noisemakers that can be used to help your puppy learn what you want her to do. When she's good, you'll

Tiny Dog + Tiny Accident = Tiny Problem?

It is harder to housetrain small dogs. Their bladders are very small and they need to go out often, but if you are a good teacher, small dogs can learn to be clean in the house, too.

Often people don't watch little dogs as carefully as they do big dogs. Anyone who has cleaned up a Great Dane's puddle will be watching closely to make sure it doesn't happen again. Wiping up a little dribble here and there from a small dog might not seem like such a big deal, but it is.

Dogs like to go in areas that smell like urine. If there's a urine spot behind your couch that you don't clean up completely, your puppy is likely to wet there again and again. She'll learn to go to the bathroom in her outdoor potty area . . . and also in her indoor potty area (perhaps one that you don't even know about). Once this becomes a habit, it is much harder to fix. Don't let it happen in your house.

Puppy Pop Quiz

Q: Do dogs dream?

A: Yes. The deepest stage of sleep is called REM (rapid eye movement), and that's when dreaming occurs. Puppies dream more than adult dogs. If you see your puppy twitching or "running" in her sleep, she's in the middle of a REM cycle. Don't wake her up; let her have her dreams.

click and give her a treat. The noise helps her figure out exactly what she did that made you happy. The clicker can be a very useful tool when housetraining your puppy. See the "Training" chapter for more information about clicker training.

Go to Bed

You can train your puppy to go into her crate by following the steps below and saying three simple words: *"Go to bed."* Of course, you can use the same steps to train your puppy to lie on a mat or bed outside of her crate as well. Be sure to use different words so your puppy will know whether you want her to go in her crate or lie on a bed outside the crate. For example, you could say, *"Go to bed"* when you want her to go into her crate and *"Settle"* when you'd like her to rest on a bed nearby.

Make sure to never push your puppy when you are training her to go into the crate. If she doesn't go in on her own, ask your parents for help.

Try It

1. Start with your treats in one hand and your clicker in the other. Stand close to your puppy's crate.
2. Toss a treat into her crate.

3. Click when she steps into the crate and eats the treat.
4. Repeat this several times so that she can practice.

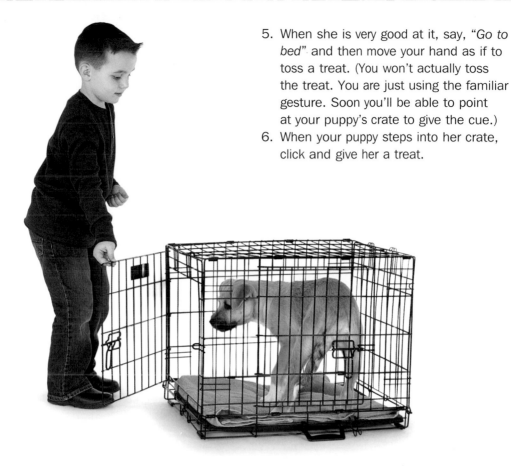

5. When she is very good at it, say, *"Go to bed"* and then move your hand as if to toss a treat. (You won't actually toss the treat. You are just using the familiar gesture. Soon you'll be able to point at your puppy's crate to give the cue.)

6. When your puppy steps into her crate, click and give her a treat.

Having Trouble?

If your puppy isn't going into her crate, you may be starting from too far away. Move closer to her crate and try the steps again.

If your puppy doesn't go into the crate without your tossing the treat, you may need to work on steps 1 through 3 for a few days to give her lots of practice.

Socialization

Wouldn't it be great if there were a magic pill that would help your puppy grow up confident and strong?

Socialization means getting used to new things. Do you remember the first time you rode an escalator? At first, many people are uncomfortable standing at the top and looking down, especially down a long escalator. But after you've ridden escalators a while, you can step on them without thinking twice. The more you do something, the easier it becomes. The same is true for puppies.

Although there's no quick fix, the things you do with your puppy can have a big effect on how she develops. If a very young puppy has fun—lots and lots of fun—with all sorts of people, sights, sounds, and surfaces, she'll learn to like them. And if she likes them, they won't scare her.

START EARLY

Bit by bit, your puppy's world is expanding. Now that she's in your home, she'll need your help because she'll be seeing new things every single day. The first 16 weeks of a puppy's life is called the "socialization window" because it's the best time for her to become familiar with people and all the things that go with them.

What's the Rush?

What's magic about these early weeks? Why is this the best time to introduce your puppy to new things?

Many kinds of animal babies don't need to know what is safe and what is dangerous. Their parents take care of them. As the babies get older, their parents teach them what they need to know.

In the early period, these babies explore without any fear. They'll walk right up and investigate. It's a great way to learn—as long as a parent is watching over them.

But from a safety perspective, it's not a good long-term plan. This is why most animals become cautious of new things as they get older. It keeps them safe. Whereas a young animal might walk right up to an unknown animal, an older animal would not. It could be a predator. Older animals take a lot more time to make up their minds about whether something new is good or bad.

This is why your puppy needs to meet many friendly people when she's young. We want her to think people are nothing surprising or unusual. They're her friends! For dogs, the first 12 weeks are the best time to meet people and learn all about us. Get busy!

During her first 16 weeks, you are helping your puppy figure out what is normal and what isn't. This is really important. Puppies who have a wide variety of good experiences grow up more comfortable and confident. Puppies who don't get this chance to explore and enjoy new things will have more trouble with change as they grow up.

Safety First

Have a good plan for keeping your puppy safe and comfortable when you are socializing her, so that she doesn't get hurt. If she were startled by a garbage truck, she could run into the street. Always use a leash when you are outdoors. When you are indoors, stay right beside her to help in case she needs you. For instance, if she peeks too far through an open staircase, she could fall.

You'll be her safety patrol, alert for danger that she doesn't know anything about.

What If My Puppy Is Older? Is It Too Late?

If your puppy is over 16 weeks old, you should absolutely still work on socialization. Every little bit helps.

Don't delay. You will find that it gets tougher with each passing week. Focus on doing as much as you can as soon as possible.

Give your older puppy lots of positive experiences with people. You'll need to take things a bit more slowly. Don't pressure her. Use lots of treats to help her love meeting people and seeing new things.

If your puppy seems very worried about things, contact a dog trainer right away. The sooner a trainer gets involved, the more he or she will be able to help you.

PUPPIES MEETING PEOPLE

Puppies need to learn that people come in all shapes and sizes. Your puppy needs to know that people not only walk upright, but also use inline skates, bikes, strollers, crutches, canes, and scooters.

A puppy with good socialization will see a person who moves in an unusual way and think, "Oh, good, a person! I should go say hi." But a puppy who hasn't had the chance to meet many people may think, "Oh, no, a monster!" Then she may try to get away or will bark at the stranger.

Socializing your puppy takes work. Ideally your puppy should meet at least 100 different people before she's 12 weeks old. This is challenging; you'll need to make an effort. Try to introduce your puppy to as many new people as you can each week.

Not only does she need to meet these people, but she needs to enjoy being with them. That's a bit trickier. Friends and neighbors may rush over to ask if they can meet your puppy. Puppies are so cute that people want to hug and cuddle them. That can be a bit much for a puppy.

Just for Fun

Blow some bubbles for your puppy. Does she like to pop them or do they make her nervous? How old she is the first time she gets to see bubbles may affect whether she thinks they are scary or fun.

Is she loose and wiggly or showing stress signals? (See the chapters on "Canine Communication" and "How to Behave Around Dogs" to learn about the signals she'll use.)

Let her approach or move away on her own terms. If she doesn't feel pressured, she will find that strangers are friendly people who offer yummy treats. Then she'll look forward to meeting new people.

In addition to learning about people, your puppy should explore sights, sounds, and surfaces. She should learn about cars, vacuums, and stairs. Try to think of all the things she'll see in her life and, if possible, let her learn about them before she's 12 weeks old in a positive, but not overwhelming way.

Always have your treat bag filled with delicious tidbits when you take your puppy out. Offer people treats, and ask them to encourage your puppy to come closer to get a treat.

Don't just pick your puppy up and hand her to a stranger. Let her be in control. Whenever you are out with your puppy, watch her body language.

Good and Bad Responses

Let's say your puppy sees something that could be scary, like a lawn mower, a vacuum, a flag flapping in the wind, or a person wearing a funny hat. Check out her body language. How is she doing? How can you help her?

Poor Responses	What You Should Do
Your puppy won't eat. She doesn't move around much and isn't interested in exploring.	When your puppy is this stressed, she's not learning good things. In fact, a bad experience could cause her to be more fearful in the future.
Your puppy is trying to get away. She may pull to the end of her leash, try to go under bushes, or struggle if you hold her.	Move away (or move the scary thing away). Distance will help.
Your puppy is too revved up and is barking or lunging at the flag. She's very focused on it and isn't paying any attention to you.	Check to see if your puppy can relax and have fun farther way. If so, practice there. If not, make a plan for next time. What can you do to make it less scary for your puppy?
Good Response	**What You Should Do**
Your puppy is exploring. She's relaxed and interested in her environment. She'll eat the treats you offer and pays only a little bit of attention to the new thing.	Stay with her and have fun.

PUPPIES MEETING PUPPIES

Playing with other dogs is something many puppies enjoy. If you are looking for playmates for your puppy, keep these tips in mind:

- Always have an adult supervise when your puppy is playing with others.
- Puppies under 16 weeks should play mostly with other puppies.

Scavenger Hunt

Plan a field trip with your family and go on a scavenger hunt to try to find these people or items in your neighborhood. Check each one that you find. The more of them your puppy happily investigates, the more socialized your puppy will be.

People

❏ An infant held by an adult
❏ An infant in a car seat
❏ A girl, between 2 and 6
❏ A boy, between 2 and 6
❏ A small group of kids (no more than 5) between 2 and 6
❏ A girl, 7 or older
❏ A boy, 7 or older
❏ A small group of kids (no more than 5) 7 or older
❏ A small group of kids playing with a ball
❏ A man with a beard (A mustache is okay if you can't find a bearded man.)
❏ A friendly stranger in a hat
❏ A friendly stranger in sunglasses
❏ A person with a bike (who stops the bike and greets the dog)
❏ A person on inline skates or a skateboard (People moving "abnormally" often worry dogs.)
❏ A person in a wheelchair
❏ A person using crutches or a cane
❏ A person in uniform
❏ A person carrying packages
❏ A person with a bag or a purse swinging from his or her arm
❏ A woman wearing a flowing skirt or dress

Sights, Sounds, Sensations, and Surfaces

❏ A stroller
❏ A balloon
❏ An umbrella
❏ An automatic door
❏ A mirror
❏ A bus (loading/unloading passengers)
❏ A grocery cart moving past you and your dog
❏ Walking between two parked cars
❏ A cat
❏ An older, well-socialized dog (meeting off leash in a neutral, safe area)
❏ A pet store
❏ Flapping movement, such as a flag or shaking out a towel
❏ A sudden soft noise, such as a magazine dropping
❏ A sudden louder noise, such as dropping keys
❏ A sudden scary noise, such as a pan dropping (Use a helper so the dog doesn't associate this with you.)
❏ A gravel road
❏ Tile floors
❏ Sand
❏ Mud
❏ Bathtub (first without water, then damp, then with an inch of water)
❏ A lawn mower
❏ A sprinkler

Remember, this is just a starting point. What other things can you find for your puppy to enjoy?

- A good dog-training class—where vaccination records are required—is the best place to introduce your puppy to other dogs and puppies.
- Break up play frequently so your puppy doesn't get overexcited.
- Not all adult dogs enjoy puppies. If an adult dog shows signs of avoidance (such as stiffening, turning away, or showing teeth), choose a different playmate for your puppy.
- Let your puppy get used to new dogs slowly.
- If your puppy seems scared to play with other puppies, seek assistance from a positive dog trainer.

TOO CLOSE FOR COMFORT

Physical space is important to people. We get a lot closer to our family and friends than we do to people we don't know. We'll stand close to strangers in a crowded elevator, but the moment the doors open, we step off and move apart.

People don't like the feeling of being trapped near someone or something that makes them uncomfortable. We feel better when we have enough space to move around freely.

Dogs pay a lot of attention to space, too. Whenever your puppy seems worried or uncomfortable, one of the best things to do is add distance. Distance makes scary things less scary.

If your puppy is worried about a truck, move farther down the street. If she doesn't like the helium balloon in your living room, move it into the next room and find a way to get her used to it before you bring it closer.

How far should you go? There's no magic distance. Watch your puppy's body language. When she loosens up and acts more like herself, you'll know she's no longer "too close for comfort."

Don't worry that you are babying her. By giving her enough space, you'll teach her that the scary things aren't so scary. Then you can encourage her to come closer at her own pace. With your help, her comfort zone will grow to include many things.

Dog Math: If It Doesn't Add Up . . .

Dogs like everything to make sense. If something doesn't seem right, they will become suspicious and nervous.

For example, if your puppy sees you in a bike helmet, she may think

SOUNDS LIKE YOU AND SMELLS LIKE YOU, BUT DOES NOT LOOK LIKE YOU = IT'S NOT YOU.

Part of your socialization job is to let your puppy know that people can vary. We may wear heavy winter coats, carry odd-shaped packages, or have a raspy voice from a cold, but we're all still friendly people.

No Teasing

It's never okay to deliberately startle or scare a puppy. Some people think it's funny. They might use a vacuum very close to a puppy who is afraid of it. Then they laugh when the puppy barks or runs away.

That's not funny; it's mean. Teasing a puppy won't help her become braver. It will make her more afraid.

As her best friend, it's your job to protect her from anyone who doesn't understand that.

Canine Communication

To be your puppy's best friend, you have to learn to "speak dog" so that you can understand what she's thinking and feeling.

WHAT TO LOOK FOR

It's easy to spot when a puppy is happy. But how do you know when she is stressed? What signals are you looking at?

When a dog is happy, she will have a relaxed face with an open mouth, like a smile with her chin slightly up. Now, look at the photos below of a child and a puppy. When they are less comfortable, each one has his neck angled slightly downward and his mouth closed.

They are using body language, which is a way of showing how you feel without talking. Body language happens naturally, without your even thinking about it. You don't decide *how* to look happy or sad, you just do. Your emotions affect your appearance.

People use a lot of body language. Dogs do, too. In fact, it's your puppy's main way of communicating. Her facial expressions and body positions tell you how she is feeling. Although people's faces and bodies are very different from dogs', our body language is similar in many ways.

It's important to pay attention to your puppy's body language. By noticing signals and paying attention to what they mean, you'll have a much better relationship with your

puppy. Your puppy will be happy knowing she can rely on you in stressful situations.

STRESSFUL MOMENTS

No one is happy all the time. Just as you have different moods throughout the day, so will your puppy. That sounds pretty clear, but a lot of people don't realize it. Many people talk as if dogs feel the same way all the time. They'll say things like, "Oh, I have a good dog. She loves everyone and would never growl."

That's not fair. We sometimes have unrealistic expectations for dogs, and we expect them to be comfortable in all situations. But there are lots of times people feel uncomfortable, nervous, or afraid. When we are stressed, we can become crabby or irritable. Your puppy might have times when she feels crabby, too.

Imagine that you have a book report due for school on Monday. On Friday afternoon, you decide to play outside because you have plenty of time to do the project over the weekend. On Saturday, you forget all about it. Two hours before bedtime on Sunday, you suddenly remember. Your father is annoyed and says, "You had all weekend to work on this. Why are you

What About Eyebrows?

Make a happy face. Now try to look angry. How about sad? For each expression, you probably moved your eyebrows. Dogs do, too.

Many dogs have eyebrows that are a different color from the surrounding fur. These markings help make the dog's expressions more obvious. Since dogs are social animals, being able to read each other's expressions is an important skill.

Do your puppy's eyebrows stand out from the rest of her face?

just getting started now? You really need to manage your homework better. It's your responsibility."

You settle in at the kitchen table and get to work. After working for an hour, you are getting close to finished when your little sister comes and sits beside you at the table. She keeps talking and it's distracting you. You ask her to stop, but she doesn't. Instead, she gets a cup of milk and says she's going to help you glue pictures to the pages. However, as she reaches for your glue stick, she knocks over her milk and it spills all across the table, soaking the pages of your book report. Now you'll have to start over again!

Maybe you would yell. You wouldn't really mean to. When you feel stressed and frustrated, you don't use your best behavior.

Similarly, your puppy may find herself in a tough situation. If you don't know how to read and understand her body language, she, too, may have a bad reaction.

The 5 F's of Stress

Everybody has heard about fight and flight (the urge to either attack or run away in a stressful situation). These are two common reactions to stress, but they aren't the only ones. When people or animals find themselves in a tough spot, most responses will fall within one of these groups.

1. **Fight.** This doesn't have to mean physical violence. It includes talking back, making threatening gestures, or standing your ground. Telling your sister that you'll hide all of her Legos if she doesn't stop coming in your room is a "fight" response.

2. **Flight.** Any attempt to get away, from slowly slinking out of a room to full-scale running, counts as flight. Even looking away in the hopes that Great Aunt Edna won't ask you to come tell her all about school would count as "flight."

3. **Faint.** This is very uncommon in dogs. (In fact, if your dog ever faints, you should take her to the veterinarian for a checkup right away.) But many people faint at the sight of blood—even when it isn't their own—and opossums are known for "playing dead" after fainting.

4. **Freeze.** Both dogs and people often freeze in a stressful situation. It's like the moment when the teacher calls your name to come up and deliver a report in front of the whole class, and, for a second, you can't move. Rabbits often freeze, and when you start watching for it, you'll see that dogs do, too. This can be easy to miss, but it's a great signal to note.

5. **Fooling Around.** Sometimes there's too much behavior and it serves as a distraction. (It also provides a physical outlet for some of the body's stress.) A friendly dog meeting someone who makes her nervous may act extra silly, by jumping around or tugging on her leash. Like when you are trying not to tell a friend about a surprise, you may find yourself saying all sorts of things you wouldn't ordinarily say because you are trying to keep the secret.

THE RANGE OF BEHAVIOR

The simplest way to learn how to recognize your puppy's different moods is to think of behavior as having three categories: green, yellow, and red—like a traffic light.

The green zone is enjoyment. Your puppy feels safe and happy and wants to continue what she's doing. For many puppies, playing in the yard is something they really enjoy.

The yellow zone is tolerance. Your puppy can handle what's going on, but she doesn't

A Moment of Doubt

When your puppy is unsure about something, give her some time to figure it out. Don't rush her. Two signals that will help you recognize these unsure moments are a tilted head or a slightly raised front paw.

Your puppy may tilt her head to one side when she is confused or trying to figure something out. Dogs look very cute when they do this.

When your puppy lifts her front paw a little, it may mean she is worried or unsure.

really like it. Given a choice, she'd prefer to do something else.

The red zone is called "enough already" because your puppy really wants to stop what is happening. She may try to walk away or avoid a situation, and in especially bad moments, she may even grumble or growl to tell you she feels uncomfortable.

Are We Having Fun?

Sometimes when you are playing together, you may not be sure if your puppy is having fun. To test this, stop and stay perfectly still. If your puppy tries to get you to "wake up" and play again, she was having fun. If she moves on to another activity, you know she was ready for a change.

puppy a little. When you see these signals, ask yourself if there is something you can do to help your puppy relax. Sometimes it may be best to give her a little rest period.

Green Zone = Enjoyment

When your puppy is happy, her body will be loose and wiggly. In fact, you may even see her moving more from left to right than forward. Her mouth will be open much of the time, but she won't be panting.

Yellow Zone = Tolerance

The yellow zone is filled with important signals that tell you it's time to help your

- **Lip Licking.** Your puppy will quickly flick her tongue out and lick her lips and nose. This often happens several times in a row. Think of it as the doggy version of thumb sucking.
- **Half-Moon Eyes.** The "half moon" refers to the white crescent shape that shows at the corner of your puppy's eyes when she is a little stressed. This is an easy signal to spot, once you know how to look for it. (A few breeds, like Boston Terriers, always show white around the edges of their eyes.)
- **Closed Mouth.** When your puppy is tense, she'll close her mouth. When she relaxes, she'll open it. Watch for this; it's a great way to figure out how comfortable your puppy is with something new.

PARENT BOX:

Was that a Bite?

Any dog can bite, regardless of breed type. When working with your puppy, it's important to distinguish between normal puppy mouthing and more deliberate nipping, which may be caused by over-excitement or asking the puppy to do something she doesn't like.

If your puppy is older than 4 months and still seems quite mouthy, contact a trainer to help you resolve the problem. If not addressed, these nips could become bites in the future. Early intervention can keep a small problem from becoming a big one.

A BODY LANGUAGE EXPERIMENT

Imitate these poses. Changing your body language can affect your mood. How do you feel in each posture?

Try to match the following emotions with the pictures: Upset, Sad, Happy, Worried. Check the Answer Key below to see if you got them right!

1. Close your mouth. Make your eyes wide and look to the side.

2. Tilt your head to one side and rest it against something. Close your mouth. Draw your eyebrows up and slightly together. Breathe slowly and deeply.

3. Lean forward, open your mouth wide, and wrinkle your nose. Stare at something.

4. Tilt your head to the side, look off into the distance, and open your mouth.

Answer Key 1. Worried, 2. Sad, 3. Upset, 4. Happy

Red Zone = Enough Already

The signals in the red zone tell you that your puppy is very stressed and wants to end the interaction.

- **Trying to Get Away or Hiding.** Pay attention when your puppy tries to get away from something or hides. Make sure she can safely get to a place where she feels comfortable. Don't force her to stay in a scary situation.
- **Fear Crouch.** Sometimes when a dog is overwhelmed and afraid, she will lie down

- **Yawning.** By giving a big yawn, your puppy can stretch her jaw and relax her face. People often hold tension in their jaws, too. Have you ever clenched your teeth when riding your bike down a steep hill?
- **Turning Away.** Your puppy may turn away or even pretend she doesn't notice something stressful. Imagine being at a party where you see a woman who loves to hug you, even though you don't know her very well. It makes you uncomfortable. Would you try to look away and hope that she didn't notice you? Sometimes dogs will do that, too.
- **Shaking Off.** Your puppy will shake off when she's wet, but she'll also do it just after a stressful experience. Pay attention when you see a dry dog shake off. Something stressful happened in the last minute or so. For example, it may happen right after several friends pet your puppy. Ask your friends not to get too excited around your puppy, because it could be too much for her.

By noticing these signals, you'll learn to know when your puppy is uncomfortable. You'll be able to keep your puppy feeling safe, happy, and understood.

Do's and Don'ts for Helping Your Puppy

Imagine standing on the edge of a diving board and wanting to jump off. All of your friends have done it, and now they want you to do it, too. You are a little scared, but you'd like to try. What might help you feel ready to try it? What might make you more nervous?

Here are some ideas for helping your puppy when she gets nervous:

- Be calm and quiet. Don't shout or get too excited.
- Use treats to help your puppy enjoy what is happening. Reward her for each little part.
- Give your puppy space. Don't let people crowd around her, and keep your face away from hers.
- Don't push or pull your puppy to get her to do something.
- Take things slowly. Let your puppy walk away and come back when she's ready to try again.

PARENT BOX:

Do Not Punish Grumbles and Growls

It's tempting to correct a dog for growling, especially at a child. Don't do it! By the time you hear a growl, many earlier, more subtle signals have been missed and the dog is showing extreme distress.

Figure out what the problem is and fix it. Punishment may rid you of the warning signal, but it does not resolve the basic problem (e.g., the puppy being nervous when a child tries to carry her or feeling uncomfortable with rough handling). Instead you may wind up with a dog who bites without warning, which is definitely not what you want.

The signals in the yellow zone are your cues for what to look for and when to intervene. By watching carefully and addressing any concerns as they develop, you can prevent your dog from feeling the need to grumble or growl.

in an attempt to defuse the situation. Do not touch a dog in a fear crouch.

- **Growling.** Growling is the canine equivalent of yelling at someone. If your puppy growls, it means she's been pushed over the edge. Some puppies growl when they are uncomfortable with being touched or when they have something they don't want you to take away.

If you see any of these signals, ask your parents to help your puppy.

Escape and Avoidance

When a dog grumbles or growls, people understand that she is having a problem, but the red zone is more than just aggressive signals.

Growling is rare in puppies. Dogs grow *into* aggression. The things that a puppy does not feel comfortable with are often the things that make an adult dog growl or snap.

Most puppies will try to get away from things that make them uncomfortable. Pay attention and help your puppy get somewhere she feels safe.

Tail Wagging

Many people believe that a wagging tail means a dog is happy and friendly. This is not always true.

There are many different kinds of wags. As you get better at reading body language, you'll learn to recognize some different wags in your puppy. Friendly wags are usually low and wide. Sometimes your puppy's whole body will wiggle in excitement.

When a dog is on alert, her tail position is likely high and somewhat stiff. Usually this wag will be faster and not very wide.

How To Behave Around Dogs

Now that you know a little about how dogs use body language, you will be better able to communicate with them. It's tempting to believe that every dog would like to be petted and played with, but that's not true.

Dogs are like people. Some are very social and outgoing. They like a lot of attention. Other dogs are shy until you get to know them, and prefer to interact only with family and close friends. By understanding body language, you'll be able to show dogs that you are friendly, and you'll also be able to tell whether a dog wants to interact with you.

People often believe that petting a dog is a good way to make friends, but is it? Would you like someone you just met to play with your hair or give you a big hug? Probably not. Take your time when you meet a new dog.

MEETING A NEW DOG

When you meet a new dog—and when your friends come to meet your puppy—it's best to follow three rules:

1. Ask the owner.
2. Ask the dog.
3. If both the owner and the dog say it's okay, pet the dog appropriately.

When you see a dog you'd like to meet, the first thing you should do is stand still. Don't move toward the dog. Rushing toward a dog could startle or frighten her.

Stop at least 5 feet (1.5 m) away and ask the owner if you can meet the dog. Be prepared for the answer to be no. Some dogs don't want to meet new people.

If the owner says you may meet the dog, you should next ask the dog. Since dogs don't use words, you'll have to use body language to communicate.

Still standing a distance away, extend your fist slowly toward the dog. This is not a punching motion. All you are doing is extending a body part so that the dog can approach and sniff if she chooses to do so.

Avoiding Hurt Feelings

Dogs say no for all sorts of reasons, and it isn't really about you; it's about them.

Have you ever told a friend that you can't play? Maybe it's time for dinner or your grandmother is visiting or you have too much homework. You aren't saying to the friend, "I don't like you;" you're saying, "Not right now."

If either the owner or the dog says no, please don't take it personally. No one is saying that you aren't a good friend for dogs, only that, at this moment, it's not a good time to pet this dog.

There are many puppies and dogs who enjoy meeting new people. Keep practicing your skills and you'll have many chances to meet social dogs.

Talk sweetly to her. She won't understand your words, but she'll recognize your friendly tone.

Watch her body language carefully. If she turns her head away or moves farther from you, that tells you that she is not interested in visiting right now.

If she's curious about you, she may approach to sniff your hand. This is a "maybe" answer, but you need to wait for a "yes" before you pet the dog.

If a dog seems unsure, try turning sideways and alternating between glancing at the dog and looking away. Keep your expression soft and friendly. Wait to see if she will come to you.

A dog saying "yes" will come close to you and will be loose and wiggly. She may nudge gently at your hands and will often rub her face or shoulders against you.

If the dog wants to be petted, turn your fist over and gently scratch the dog beneath her chin. Many dogs like being scratched on the chin, neck, shoulders, and ribs.

Avoid the dog's sensitive eyes and ears. Reaching over to pet the top of her head would make her uncomfortable. She'd probably lift her chin up to watch your hand as it goes over her head.

Tails are also off limits when you first meet a dog, but once the dog is comfortable with you, she may enjoy having her hips scratched.

Be careful that you don't frighten a dog by looming over her. It's easy to do since

When a Dog Barks

Never touch a barking dog—even your own dog. When a dog is barking, she is focused on something. If you touch her, you could startle her, and she could react badly. If your puppy is barking, try calling her or throwing a toy to distract her. If you can't get her attention, ask an adult to help.

A Doggy Hello

When dogs greet one another, they usually go through a standard greeting ritual. A polite greeting starts with the dogs approaching one another from an angle. A direct approach is less polite.

The dogs will sniff noses and then sniff necks. Finally they'll sniff each other's rear end. People think that's rude, but it's not rude in dog language. It's an important part of the greeting ritual.

After your puppy has had a moment to sniff the other dog's nose, neck, and rear, use your voice—not your leash—to call your puppy away.

Often older dogs don't want to meet puppies, so be sure that you let your puppy approach only dogs who show signs of being interested in meeting her.

people are so much taller than most dogs, but it can make dogs very uncomfortable.

HELPING YOUR PUPPY MEET YOUR FRIENDS

Puppies are irresistible. Your friends will all want to come over to meet and play with your puppy. This can be wonderful fun for all of you if it's done right.

Because kids and dogs communicate so differently, we can sometimes have bad situations even when everyone has good intentions. Having two, three, or four kids clustered around can overwhelm a puppy. Watch your puppy's body language to make sure she's happy and relaxed.

Take turns petting the puppy. It can be fun to sit in a circle and call the puppy from person to person. If each person gives your

Most Dog Bites Are Preventable

It may surprise you to learn that dogs bite people they know more often than they bite strangers. Every bite is the result of a miscommunication. Dogs bite when they are uncomfortable, frightened, or angry, and when people don't understand their signals.

Knowing how to read body language will help keep you safe. When you are with your puppy or other dogs, ask yourself often which emotional zone the dog is in: Enjoyment, Tolerance, or Enough Already?

Pay particular attention to dogs showing tolerance. Can you make things better? Or is it time to give the dog some space and down time?

These are the three most important things to remember:

1. Dogs don't like hugs and kisses. This is a classic human/canine miscommunication. Don't let a dog feel trapped when you are trying to show love. This is especially important to remember with dogs you don't know well, but it's true for your puppy as well.
2. Give dogs lots of space when they are on their beds, in their crates, tethered outdoors, or eating/chewing something. Make sure the dog understands that you are not a threat.
3. Be a tree when a dog makes you uncomfortable or seems too excited. Stand still, fold your arms in front of your body, be quiet, and wait. When it is safe to do so, slowly and calmly walk away.

puppy a treat when she comes over, she'll really enjoy the game. Play for only 10–15 minutes and then give your puppy a nap in her crate, so that she can rest up and play some more.

WHEN YOU ARE UNCOMFORTABLE

There may be times when you are uncomfortable with a dog. Since dogs communicate almost entirely through body language, that's the best way for you to communicate with them, too.

Use body language if you want to tell a dog to go away. Stand with your feet hip-width apart and firmly planted so that you are well balanced and sturdy. Clasp your hands together and hold them down in front of your body. Look down at the ground. This is called being a tree. When being a tree, you are being very still and avoiding all eye contact with the dog.

Dogs find this pretty boring. When you stand like a tree, typically they'll take a quick sniff and move on. Most dogs will be calmer in the presence of a child who is being still than around one who is interacting.

If you see a dog out loose when you are out with your friends, you could all stand like a tree. If the dog approaches you, stay in your tree position. Most times the dog will just take a quick sniff and move away. If you jerk or move or make noises, the dog will be interested and stay longer, so be very still and very quiet. Most dogs will move away quickly.

Puppy Pop Quiz

Q: Why do dogs bark so much?

A: Wolves rarely bark, but dogs often bark, usually for one of these reasons:
1. To alert others to something out of the ordinary
2. To communicate a message, such as barking in distress when left alone
3. To express excitement

Some breeds are more likely to bark than others. Be sure to socialize your dog well and give her lots of exercise so that her barking doesn't become a problem.

Hugs

It's tempting to hug, kiss, and squeeze a puppy. This kind of physical affection is normal for people, but not for dogs. It makes them feel trapped and uncomfortable. Many dogs learn to tolerate being hugged—and even know that the people intend it kindly—but very few dogs enjoy it.

Instead of hugging, practice petting dogs with slow, smooth strokes.

Being a tree is not only for when you encounter a dog who is a little scary. You can also use it with dogs who are too excited or too friendly.

It's a great thing to do when you go to the house of a friend whose dog gets too excited at the door. When the dog is jumping around, very happy that you've arrived, you can simply stand like a tree until he settles. This is a good time for a parent to help too.

And if you ever accidentally get your puppy too riled up, you can be a tree so that she understands it is time to settle down again.

Always think about what message your body language is sending to dogs, and you'll find that many more dogs will be comfortable with you.

How to Keep Your Puppy Out of Trouble

Your puppy's idea of good manners may not match yours. It's perfectly normal for dogs to dig, chew, bark, and jump on people. Most families, however, don't want their dogs to behave this way. Your puppy will need your help to learn what's expected of her.

Think of your puppy like a toddler. She'll have the ability to get into things, but no sense of right and wrong—or even safe and unsafe. So, just as you would for a toddler, you'll have to help a lot. Keep things she shouldn't have out of her reach. If she finds something you missed, give her a toy to play with and gently take away (and then put away) whatever she found.

Be patient with her. She needs your help. Planning ahead will help you avoid problems. Everyone in the family plays a role. Don't leave this up to your parents.

EXERCISE

Most dog breeds were developed with specific jobs in mind, such as hunting, shepherding farm animals, and guarding property. They are athletes and need exercise.

Today, only a small percentage of dogs do the work they were bred for. Most family dogs don't have such active lives. They go for walks, greet guests, and take trips to the park, but much of their time is spent just hanging out with the family. In some ways, this is like driving a racecar to the

Is Your Puppy Part Goat?

Goats will eat almost anything. Some puppies will, too. Here's a list of items that your puppy might try to eat, but shouldn't. Remember that it's your job to keep your puppy from getting into things she shouldn't.

- Baskets
- Car keys
- Cat poop
- Cell phones
- Crayons, pencils, and pens
- Deck of cards
- Door frames
- Grass
- Homework
- Library books
- Lip balm
- Loaf of bread
- Money
- Photos
- Rocks
- Ropes
- Stuffed animals
- Toys

Puppy Pop Quiz

**Q: Who has more teeth:
a person or a dog?**

A: Dogs. Adult dogs typically have 42 teeth. Humans get 32, but many people have their wisdom teeth (back molars that teens develop) removed, which leaves only 28. Your puppy's four long pointy teeth are called canines. You also have four teeth called canine teeth. They're the pointiest ones. Smile. Can you see them?

grocery store: lots of power and energy, but no way to use it up.

If you get a puppy with lots of energy, you'll need to be sure that you give her plenty of exercise. Her exercise needs will increase month by month. Most puppies need at least three 20-minute sessions of very active play each day in addition to the time spent walking and training them.

Time spent alone in a fenced-in yard does not count as exercise. You need to be out there with her, encouraging her to be active—and ensuring that she's not eating acorns or chewing the fence posts. Teach your puppy to play fetch so that she can run after toys you throw.

Rest

After all that exercise, your puppy will need a nap. Be sure that your puppy spends time in her crate resting and recharging so that she'll be ready to play again later.

Just like people, puppies can get cranky when they're overtired. When she's resting, leave your puppy alone.

TIME-OUTS

When your puppy keeps doing something that you do not want her to do, you can give her a short time-out. If she's in a safe spot, get up and leave her there alone. If you can't leave her where she is, put her in her crate.

Either way, she'll learn that if she does that behavior, she loses you. And since you are building a great relationship, she won't want to lose you.

The most effective time-outs are well timed. Ideally as soon as she makes the

mistake, you'll say "Whoopsie!" and walk out. Go so fast that it startles her. Then walk around for 15–30 seconds before you go back to her.

Keep time-outs short. The real lesson comes in the first few seconds. If you leave her for several minutes, she'll have time to start thinking about other things. You definitely don't want to come back from a time-out to find her happily chewing on something she shouldn't. That would be a lesson for you—not for her!

Don't Hold a Grudge

Keep in mind that your puppy is not trying to upset you. She didn't shred your book report because she wanted to make you mad; she did it because you left the papers where she could reach them and, well, shredding is fun!

Forgive but don't forget. Instead make a plan to prevent it from happening again.

Just for Fun

Give your puppy an empty water bottle or milk jug with a handful of kibble in it. She'll have fun batting it around to get the food out. Be sure to take it away from her when it's empty so that she doesn't chew the plastic.

Puppy Pop Quiz

Q: Why do scenthounds have long ears?

A: It makes sense that bloodhounds, bassets, and other scenthounds often have very big noses—"the better to smell you with, my dear"—but why do they have such long ears? Many people believe that the long ears help trap odors, which makes it easier for the dog to track and identify them. Those long ears don't help the dogs hear better; they help them smell better. Amazing!

CHEW TOYS

Your puppy's job is to chew. Your job is to teach her what to chew. Buy a few hollow, hard rubber toys that you can stuff with things to chew. At first, you can make these simple by filling them with kibble that will easily fall out.

As your puppy learns how to remove the contents, make the toys more challenging. For example, you could fill a toy with some peanut butter, add some dog treats, put a glob of applesauce in to fill the empty spaces, and then freeze the toy. When it's ready, your puppy will have a frozen snack to enjoy.

I'm Bored

When you are bored, you have lots of options. You can read a book, draw a picture, play outside, call a friend, write an e-mail, go for a bike ride, make a snack, watch TV, or play a game.

How many choices does your puppy have?

When she's bored, she'll look around for something interesting to do, but she'll evaluate her options by dog standards. To a puppy, pulling all the stuffing out of a pillow sounds like great fun. She'd also enjoy chewing your shirt, shredding the newspaper, digging in the garden, and tugging on the cord that hangs down from a table lamp.

It's up to you to give your puppy lots of safe, fun things that she can do to keep her brain and body busy.

Chewing these kinds of toys gives your puppy a little physical exercise and some mental exercise as well. Be creative. You can stuff these kinds of toys with healthful leftovers, training treats, and dog food to come up with interesting and challenging combinations.

Do not give your puppy old shoes or knotted socks to play with. She won't know the difference between the ones she's allowed to have and the ones she is not.

TETHERS

Tethers can be very helpful for teaching a puppy how to behave. A tether is a leash or rope used to limit where your puppy can go. Loop a leash around the leg of your desk and attach it to your puppy's collar when you are doing homework. Attach a tether to your couch, so that your puppy can lie on the floor beside you (with a chew toy) while you watch TV. She'll be learning how to be calm and relaxed while hanging out with the family.

Puppy Pop Quiz

Q: Can dogs be hypoallergenic (able to be tolerated by people with allergies)?

A: No dogs can be truly considered hypoallergenic. People who are allergic to dogs react to their dander and saliva, which all dogs have. However, many allergy sufferers find that certain breeds of dogs produce dander in levels low enough not to set off an allergic reaction. These dogs often have low-shedding coats. Bathing a dog frequently and vacuuming daily also help minimize allergic reactions.

You can even wear a leash around your waist and tether your puppy to you. This way she'll always be close by as you move around the house.

Sandbox

If your puppy likes to dig, be sure to go outside with her so you can distract her if necessary. Consider giving her a sandbox to dig in. Bury some toys and treats in it for her to dig up. This may help prevent her from digging up your flowers.

PREVENTING MISTAKES

Imagine that you opened the drawer where you keep silverware and found some candy. This unexpected surprise would have you checking the silverware drawer often in the hopes of finding another treat. But you've never actually found candy in your silverware drawer, so when you are looking for a snack, you don't check that drawer. Instead you look in the cabinets where you've found food in the past.

It's the same with your puppy. If one day she discovers a sandwich within her reach and eats it, she'll look every time she comes

The Guilty Look

Dogs have simple emotions. They feel joy, fear, and anger, but they don't feel guilt or spite.

Don't be fooled by a "guilty look." Sometimes people punish their dogs, believing "she knows what she did was wrong." Nope. The guilty look is actually your puppy looking worried because of how you are behaving. If your puppy tips over a plant while you're outside and you return an hour later and act upset, she won't understand why you are acting that way. She may even make a negative association between the members of your family and certain objects. For example, she may learn that **YOU + OVERTURNED PLANT = BAD NEWS**. This negative connection may not stop her from tipping over the plants. For her to learn that lesson, you would need to be there when she did it so you could correct her right away. If not, she might learn to fear an overturned plant even if someone else knocks it over.

Don't let this happen to your relationship with your puppy. If you aren't there when she tips over the plant, don't correct her. It's best to prevent this from happening by puppy proofing the house a little better to keep her from getting into plants or similar items in the first place.

Puppy Smoothies

Frozen treats feel great on your puppy's sore gums and also keep her busy longer. Mix a few of these ingredients together in a bowl and pour them into several hollow rubber toys. Then put the toys in the freezer for a few hours. Whenever you want a healthful chew toy for your puppy, just grab a frozen treat from the freezer.

- Plain yogurt
- Bananas
- Apple chunks (remove the seeds)
- Blueberries
- Strawberries
- Sweet potato
- Peanut butter
- Canned pumpkin (not pumpkin pie filling)
- Green beans
- Water or soup broth

Buy several stuffable toys and fill them all at once. If you must hunt for a toy and then take time to stuff it, you won't use them as often as you should.

Be careful not to give grapes or raisins to your puppy. These can make her very sick.

in the room for a while. If she doesn't find anything else, she'll stop checking. But if every now and then, she finds a delicious surprise, she'll be a lifetime gambler, always hoping to score something special.

If you keep your counters and tables free of food, your puppy won't learn to counter-surf. As she ages, she won't be checking out the table every time she enters the room, because she'll believe that there's nothing there for her. When she's older, you may be able to leave things out because she won't have the habit of checking and she won't think that she's allowed to take things from the counter.

Your puppy will learn good household manners much faster if you can prevent accidental learning.

MAKE A PLAN

Whenever your puppy makes the same mistake twice, sit down and think about how you are going to prevent it from happening again.

Preventing Mistakes

What Happened	What You'll Do Next Time
Housetraining accident	More potty breaks and better supervision
Chewed your shoe	Keep your shoes in the closet and give her chew toys.
Jumped on your friends	Stand on her leash to prevent her from jumping, and teach your friends to be a tree (see the chapter on "How to Behave Around Dogs").
Ran wildly through the house	Give her plenty of exercise.
Jumped up on furniture without permission	Use a baby gate to block off her access to that room when no one is in there to supervise her.

Training

You are going to have a lot of fun training your puppy. Puppies love to learn, and they're adorably cute when they figure out what you want. The more your puppy learns, the easier it will be to teach her additional skills.

Kids can be excellent dog trainers. They're often even better than their parents. To be a good trainer, you need to be

- **Patient.** Your puppy doesn't know what you want her to do. It's going to take time and practice for her to catch on.
- **Prepared.** Keep your treats ready and reward as quickly as you can. This will help your puppy learn faster.
- **Gentle.** Whenever possible, train without touching your puppy. Never yank her collar or push her into position. When your puppy is trying to learn something new, it can be very distracting to have someone touching her. (Would you want someone touching you while you tried to figure out a puzzle?)

When you want your puppy to sit, for example, it's much better to lure her into position with a treat than to push on her bottom with your hands.

- **Calm.** Train your puppy away from distractions. And make sure that you aren't being distracting either. While your puppy is learning a new skill, try not to talk or move around much. Once she's good at it, you can add distractions while she practices.
- **Creative.** If your puppy doesn't do the right thing, she's probably confused. Stop and think about it. How can you help your puppy get it right?
- **Consistent.** Use the same hand signals and words each time you ask your puppy to do something.

Your puppy will develop confidence and good manners through training. Training opens many doors for your puppy. A well-mannered dog will be included in more family activities because her behavior will be predictable and appropriate.

PARENT BOX:

Helping Your Child Be a Good Trainer

- Just as you'll do with your puppy, notice and reward what your child is doing right. Point out all the things that are going well with training.
- Do some one-on-one training with the puppy to teach her new skills. When you are working with your kids and the puppy, let the kids do most of the training.
- If your puppy doesn't do what your child asks, resist the impulse to give the cue yourself. This would seem like you are overruling, not supporting, your child. Instead, make a suggestion and ask your child to try again. Sometimes it's something as simple as "Try stepping closer" or "take your hand out of the treat bag before you give the cue."
- In a group class, let the instructor coach your child. It's often helpful if you hold the leash so that your child can work hands-free.

Your puppy will have a unique relationship with each member of your family. Encourage your kids to train the puppy so that they'll develop a strong relationship based on trust and communication.

WHAT'S A CLICKER?

A clicker is a small noisemaker that you can hold in your hand while training. When you press it, it makes a soft clicking noise.

To use a clicker for training, you'll click whenever your puppy does something right. Think of your clicker like a camera, as though you are taking pictures of your puppy being good. Each time you click, you are capturing another example of your puppy's good behavior.

Every time you click, you'll also give your puppy a treat. Very soon, she'll learn that a click means you like what she's doing. This makes it much easier for her to learn new skills because you'll be able to mark the exact second she does what you want her to do. For example, if you are trying to teach your puppy to greet people politely, you can click and treat when she

has all four paws on the floor. If she jumps up, she will not earn a click or a treat.

It's a good idea to practice a little before you start using a clicker to train your puppy. Ask one of your siblings or parents to clap their hands in a random pattern. See if you can click as soon as they clap. Once you are pretty good at clicking when they clap, ask them to try bouncing a tennis ball. Can you click the moment the ball hits the ground?

Remember that anytime you click for your puppy, she gets a treat. Even if you make a mistake, she still gets a treat. Don't worry about making mistakes. Instead focus on doing the best job you can to click when you catch her doing something right.

and smelly! Try a variety of things to find which ones work best for your puppy. Try small bits of baked chicken, tiny cubes of cheese, or little slivers of hot dogs. Keep your treats very small so that you can reward her over and over. Wear your treat bag around the house so that you'll always have a treat ready when you want one. Keep your clicker with your treat bag.

Some treats need refrigeration. Be sure to store your treats properly between training sessions.

WHEN TO ADD WORDS

Dogs and puppies learn best through body language. Your puppy will learn faster if you teach her behaviors and let her practice them a while before you add names to them. Once your puppy has practiced a new skill many times, you can begin adding a name.

GETTING STARTED

Some people spend a lot of time saying, "No, no, no" to their puppies. They have training backward. Instead of focusing on what you *don't* want your puppy to do, pay more attention to the good stuff.

Teach your puppy what you like. You can't do that just by telling her when she makes a mistake. She could make a thousand mistakes before she does what you want. Instead reward her every time she does what you like. This way she'll quickly learn how you want her to behave—and she'll also do a lot less of the things you don't like.

When you are just beginning, food is the easiest and most powerful reward to use. Your puppy needs to eat, so why not use her food to reward her for good manners?

Get a pouch to store treats or kibble in. Dogs particularly like treats that are soft

Ouch! You Got My Finger!

- Instead of holding a treat between your fingers, lay it in the palm of your hand and put your hand in front of your puppy like a plate.
- Drop the treat on the ground.
- Put the treat in a bowl and let the puppy lick it out.
- Use a wooden spoon dipped in peanut butter. You can present the spoon to your puppy to lick like a lollipop.

Be sure that your puppy is getting plenty of exercise and lots of chew toys. Many nippy puppies just have too much energy.

Sometimes your puppy may nip your finger in her haste to take a treat. Your puppy didn't mean to hurt you. She just got excited and grabbed for the treat. But it still hurts.

- Try delivering the treat from below your dog's nose instead of above it. Think of throwing a ball. Go for the underhand move rather than overhand.

To do this, first say the cue word and then lure your puppy into position. By saying the word first, you are making it easier for your puppy to notice the word and understand its meaning. If you said "*Down*" at the same time you did the luring motion, your puppy would pay attention only to your body language, which is much easier for her to understand.

It will take many repetitions before your puppy understands that your words are actually cues for her to do something. Be patient and help your puppy succeed by practicing often.

Puppy Pop Quiz

Q: Is deafness more common in black dogs or white dogs?

A: Deafness is more common in white dogs. Scientists aren't sure exactly why, but dogs who are completely or mostly white are more likely to be deaf than dogs of any other color.

Ready to test your cue word?

When you think your puppy absolutely, positively understands what a word means, go ahead and test it. For example, when you are sure that your puppy knows the word *sit*, try changing your body position when you give the verbal cue. Will your puppy sit if you are

- raising your hands over your head?
- sitting in a chair?
- leaning over as if to tie your shoe?
- standing with your back turned toward her?
- lying on the floor?
- hiding behind a door?

You'll probably find that your puppy doesn't understand the word as well as you thought she did. That's okay. It's good for you to know that your puppy is still using some body language cues in addition to your words to understand what you want.

Keep practicing your cue words (remembering to say the word *before* you make any movements) until she can pass this kind of test.

Your puppy will need lots of practice with everything she learns. It often takes more than 200 repetitions before she'll be really good at something in the house— and even more practice to be good at it out in public.

Whenever you are teaching a new skill, set your puppy up for success. Work in a quiet area. Make sure your puppy is eager, interested, and a little hungry. If she's too tired or has too much energy, she won't be able to focus. Fill your treat bag with good food and treats, and get started. Be very patient. Remember that if she can't do the full behavior, you should reward her for making progress. Once she's got it, though, don't go back to rewarding for only part of the skill.

ATTENTION GAME

Teaching your puppy to pay attention to you is the most important skill of all. After all, you can't teach her anything if you don't have her attention.

Try It

1. Hold a treat in one hand and your clicker in the other.
2. Extend the hand holding the treat out to your side where your puppy can see it.
3. Be still and don't talk to your puppy. Just wait.
4. Your puppy will probably stare at your treat hand for a while, but then she'll glance over at your face. She'll probably look a little confused.
5. As soon as she looks at you, click and give her the treat.

Having trouble?

- If your puppy is too distracted by the treat to look away, use a less exciting treat, like dog food or cereal.
- Be sure to keep your body still. If your hand is moving around, your puppy may think you are trying to lure her into a position.

Name Game Ping-Pong

Two or more people can play this game with your puppy. Make sure that each of you has treats. Don't rely on one person to be the treat keeper.

Take turns calling your puppy's name. When she looks, click and give her a treat.

Soon she'll figure out the game and will begin looking toward the next person even before she's been called. Change the order then. Whoever the puppy is not looking at will be the one to call her.

This teaches her to listen for her name and to respond quickly.

NAME GAME

We want your puppy to know that her name means "look at me." Make it a game. Give her one chance to respond. Don't call her over and over. You certainly don't want her to think her name is Penny-Penny-Penny-PENNY!!!

Try It

1. Hold a treat in one hand and your clicker in the other.
2. Say your puppy's name in a happy voice.
3. When she turns toward you, click and give her a treat.
4. If she does not look at you, immediately walk away. You don't have to go far; just make sure she knows that if you call and she doesn't look, you're not going to stick around and call again and again.

Having trouble?

- Make sure only one person is calling her at a time.

- Click and reward her as soon as she looks at you. Don't ask her to come or sit. She earns the treat simply for turning her face toward you.

LURING

Luring is used to train your puppy by teaching her to follow a treat. Your goal is to be able to move her about 3 feet (91 cm) in any direction following a small treat as a food lure. Be sure to give her the treat at the end!

Try It

1. Hold several treats in your hand and your clicker in the other.
2. Show your puppy a treat. Hold your hand at her nose level.
3. Move your hand about 2 inches (5 cm) away from her nose.
4. When she steps forward for the treat, click and give it to her.
5. Show her another treat and move your hand again.
6. Click and treat when she comes toward the treat.
7. As she gets good at this, increase the distance.
8. Try feeding her and moving your hand away quickly so that she doesn't even stop walking.

Having trouble?

- Be sure to give your puppy treats as she moves around. If you keep moving your hand away without giving her anything, she'll give up.

- If your puppy seems confused or nervous, try not to lean over her. Kneel down beside her and try to lure her back and forth from left to right in front of you.

THE BASICS

You can train your puppy to do a lot of fun things, but let's start with the basic behaviors: *sit*, *down*, *come*, and *stay*.

Sit

Teaching your puppy to *sit* can work well in many situations. When your puppy is sitting, she won't jump on your friends, or dash out the door, or grab the paper that just fell off the table.

Try It

1. Hold a treat in one hand and your clicker in the other.
2. Show your puppy the treat. Hold your hand at her nose level. (If you hold your hand too high, she may jump.)

3. Slowly move your hand toward her, up and slightly over her head.
4. As she watches the treat, she'll fold her hind legs under her body and sit down.
5. As soon as she sits, click and give her the treat.
6. Once she is good at sitting, you can add the word. First you'll say, "*Sit*," and then you'll lure her into position.

Having trouble?

- If your puppy is jumping, you are probably holding the treat too high.
- If your puppy keeps moving away, try moving your hand slowly and keeping the rest of your body still.
- Still having trouble? Try working in a corner. This will limit how much your puppy can move around and will make her more likely to sit.

Down

Ask your puppy to *lie down* when you want her to be settled and relaxed for more than 10 seconds. Encourage your puppy to lie down and relax while you do homework or watch TV.

Try It

1. Start with your puppy in a *sit*. Imagine a capital letter "L" extending down from your puppy's nose to between her front paws and then going out in front of her.

2. With several treats in your hand, slowly draw the "L" shape. Move your hand down from your puppy's nose to between her front paws.

3. Then s-l-o-w-l-y move your hand along the floor away from your puppy. How far you go depends on how long your puppy's legs are. For most puppies, you'll go between 2 and 6 inches (5–15 cm).

4. The first few times you do this, you may want to reward her for following your hand even a few inches. She'll be a little hunched over, but not lying down. That's okay. This is just the first part of the process. Since you have several treats in your hand, you can give her a reward each time she makes a little progress.

5. When she moves her front paws forward enough that her elbows touch the ground, click and give her a treat.

Having trouble?

- If your puppy stands up instead of lying down, make sure that you are moving the treat straight down first and then out from her body. If you move the treat from her nose to a spot a few inches ahead of her forepaws, she'll lean forward, lift up her hips, and then stand to reach the treat.

Does "Down" Really Mean What You Think It Means?

Make sure that each word you use has one specific meaning. Otherwise your puppy will be very confused and won't know what to do. Some people say *"Down"* and mean

- lie down on the ground.
- get off the furniture.
- stop jumping up on a guest.

What does *down* mean in your house? Be sure that everyone knows and uses the same meaning for each cue. It may be helpful to write a list of words and what they'll mean for your puppy. Post it on the refrigerator so that everyone uses the same vocabulary.

Once you are certain that you are luring her straight down, check your speed. If you go too fast, she'll be likely to pop up.

Come

Come is a lot like the Name Game, only this time your puppy needs to move toward you. If your Name Game is strong, it will be much easier to teach your puppy to come when you call. Practice this skill at least 10 times a day to make it very strong.

Rainy Day Come Game

Once the Name Game is easy, your puppy will enjoy playing the Rainy Day *Come* Game. Let's say you decide to play with your brother and your sister. Each of you should have a small cup of treats.

While your sister plays the Name Game with your puppy in the living room, you and your brother will leave the room. You'll go stand in the kitchen, and your brother can go to the hallway.

Call your puppy. While your puppy is trotting toward you, your sister will move to a different spot in the living room.

Be sure to click and treat your puppy when she gets to you. Praise her loudly so that your siblings can hear you. (If they don't hear you, they won't know when it's their turn to call the puppy.)

Next your brother can call the puppy toward the hallway. As she's going toward him, it's time for you to choose a different place to stand in the kitchen.

Your sister will take a turn calling the puppy, and your brother will move to a slightly different spot in the hallway.

The idea is that your puppy can find each of you, but has to search a little. Puppies love searching. As she gets better at the game, you can make it harder by standing out of sight or moving to a different room.

Try It

1. Have your clicker ready and your treat bag on.
2. Say your puppy's name in a happy voice and then say, *"Come"* with the same level of enthusiasm.
3. When your puppy starts moving toward you, click and hold out a treat (even if she's still across the room).

4. Give your puppy the treat when she gets to you. Don't go to her to give the treat.

Having trouble?

- If your puppy doesn't come toward you, encourage her by making kissy noises or calling "pup-pup-pup" in a happy voice.
- Try backing away from her to make it more fun.
- Start in an easy place and work your way up to more distractions.

PARENT BOX:

When Can My Child Walk the Dog Alone?

There are many things you need to think about before sending your child out on a solo walk with a dog.

- Can your child safely handle the dog, even if the dog is startled or pulls toward something? A front-clasp harness will help, but pound for pound, dogs are much stronger than children.
- Do you live in an environment that's pretty safe for a child to walk a dog? Is it rare for you to see loose dogs or dogs barking in yards? Are most cats kept inside? Is the traffic slow or are there paths available?
- Does your dog respond well to your child? Does she usually respond properly—not only in the house, but also in a distracting environment, such as when you walk together to the park?

If you can answer yes to all of these questions, then your child may be old enough to walk the dog alone.

Don't ever send a dog out on a walk with a child as a form of protection for the child. If you think either your dog or your child needs protection from anything that might startle or frighten them, then an adult should be going on the walk as well.

A Trick to Prevent Jumping

It can be tough to teach your puppy not to jump on people. If she jumps up and someone pets her, she'll soon learn to jump for attention. Many people will say they don't mind when your puppy jumps, but it's important to teach her nice manners, because people are far less patient with adult dogs who jump.

Using two leashes when you go out with your puppy can provide a simple solution. In addition to your regular leash, get an inexpensive, lightweight leash. When you are walking your dog, hold both leashes in your hand.

When you see someone approaching, drop your lightweight leash and let it drag on the ground. If the person asks to meet your puppy, stop and step on the dragging leash. Make sure your foot is close enough to your puppy that the leash isn't long enough for her to jump up. And don't forget to keep holding on to the other leash. Your puppy will learn that jumping doesn't work, but that people will give her treats and attention when she has all four paws on the ground.

Stay

For *stay* to be a useful behavior, it's best if your puppy stays still while you move around. Otherwise, what's the point? When you are teaching *stay*, focus on the three D's:

- **Distance.** How far away will you move?
- **Duration.** How long will you ask your puppy to be still?
- **Distraction level.** What else is going on while your puppy tries to stay?

It's best if you can change only one D at a time. If you want to try to go farther away (increasing distance), be quick and calm so that this *stay* exercise is not longer or more distracting.

75

The Dishwasher Challenge!

Once your puppy is pretty good at *stay*, meaning that she can stay for up to 15 seconds while you move around, you'll be ready to try the Dishwasher Challenge.

Have your puppy *stay* as you empty the dishwasher. You can do this as one very long *stay* or as a bunch of short ones.

For example, she can *stay* while you take all the bowls to the cabinet. And *stay* again while you move the plates. *Stay* while you put the pans away. And *stay* while you deal with the silverware. Reward her after each successful *stay*.

Emptying a dishwasher requires lots of body movements and noises. You pull things out, reach up and down, and move all around. It's an excellent way to practice *stays* for puppies who are ready for a challenge.

Try It

1. Ask your puppy to *sit* or *lie down*. Wait just a moment before you click and treat. That's your very first *stay*. Half a second: excellent!
2. Try it again. Ask your puppy to *sit* or *lie down*, and count silently to three before you click and treat.
3. Do lots and lots of very short *stays* until your puppy is good at them.

Don't Ruin Your Come Cue

Make sure you don't accidentally make coming to you a bad thing. Once a puppy learns to *come* reliably, people sometimes forget to make it fun and rewarding. They'll call her to trim her nails, give her a bath, or come in from outside, but she doesn't want any of those things.

If this happens regularly, the puppy may begin to ignore the *come* cue. If she's outside sniffing all the new exciting odors, she may not *come* because she doesn't want to go in yet. Make sure you practice calling your puppy to you, giving her a treat, and then letting her go play again several times before it's time to come inside.

Having trouble?

• If your puppy is having trouble, practice two-second *stays* in which you try moving your body parts one by one. For example, you could nod your head, reward your puppy, shrug your shoulders, reward your puppy, wiggle your right arm, reward your puppy, raise your left hand, reward your puppy, twist to the left, reward your puppy. You get the idea. Once she can do these *stays*, you are ready to try making them last a little longer.

LOOSE-LEASH WALKING

No one likes to be dragged around by a dog. If you teach your puppy nice leash manners while she's small, you'll save yourself lots of aggravation when she's full grown.

Stop and Smell the Roses

Your puppy wants to smell everything. Teach her to walk nicely on a leash without sniffing because it's a skill she'll need now and then, but don't make her walk this way all the time.

Be sure your puppy gets lots of chances to sniff when you take her out. If you don't let her sniff, she can't get her main source of information. She'll be particularly interested in sniffing places other dogs have been. She knows which dogs have been to a spot just by sniffing it. Imagine going for a walk blindfolded. You could do it, but it wouldn't be nearly the same experience.

Because your puppy is so interested in exploring—and smelling—her world, she'll be more focused on where she's going than how she's getting there. She may not pay much attention to you at first.

Try It

1. Take treats and practice in your yard.
2. Whenever your puppy looks up at you, give her a treat. This will teach her to check in with you often. Watch for this.
3. Try to keep the leash loose. If your puppy pulls, stop.
4. Wait for your puppy to loosen the leash, and then the two of you can move forward again.

Having trouble?

• Be ready to reward every time she glances up at you. Many people think that their puppy is so busy looking at everything else that she never checks in. Not true! But if you aren't ready to reward her with a smile and a treat, she may think that you don't care whether she checks in or not.

Puppy Pop Quiz

Q: Can dogs get goose bumps?

A: Sort of. Goose bumps are the bumps that can appear on your skin when you get cold or frightened. Basically the muscles underneath the hair follicles of your skin contract, which makes the skin bumpy and the hair stand up a bit.

When dogs are angry or frightened, this happens to them as well, but it's much more obvious because they have so much hair. The hair on the back of a dog's neck, shoulders, and even haunches can stand on end when a dog is frightened. We usually say the dog has "raised hackles." This makes the dog seem larger and more intimidating.

It's not just dogs and people. Lots of animals experience this. If a hedgehog gets frightened, he'll roll into a ball and the muscles on his back will contract, making all those spines stand on end.

DROP IT

Puppies pick up all sorts of things. Your puppy will be interested in the TV remote control, dirty laundry, garbage, your homework, and much more. She'll want to carry and chew them all. This means that you need to teach her to give you what's in her mouth.

Practice this with toys before you try it with other things.

Try It

1. Start with a long toy. Take hold of one end as your puppy holds the other in her mouth.
2. Show her a smelly treat with your other hand.
3. Tell her *"Drop it."*
4. When she lets go of the toy, immediately give her the treat.
5. After she takes the treat, encourage her to grab hold of the toy again. This teaches her that it's a game and that she doesn't need to hide things she finds.
6. Repeat the process several times, showing her a treat, asking her to *drop it*, giving her the treat, and letting her take the toy again.

PARENT BOX:

Preventing Resource Guarding

Some dogs will behave aggressively to protect food or other valuable items. This behavior has both genetic and environmental causes.

The tricky part is that the dog gets to decide what is valuable. Often it's something that seems trivial to us, like a used tissue or food wrapper.

To help prevent resource guarding, do not allow your children to take food from the puppy. Instead, with your supervision, you can have your child approach the puppy while she's eating and toss a small, delicious treat into the bowl. This way the puppy learns that a person approaching signals good things rather than something to worry about.

If you see any troubling signs—eating faster, stiffening, staring, or growling—contact a trainer immediately. A puppy won't grow out of this. Without intervention, this behavior will get worse.

7. When she's good at this, try it with other toys as well.

8. When she has an item she should not have, DO NOT CHASE HER! Show her a treat and tell her to *drop it*.

9. When she drops the item and eats the treat, decide whether it's safe to give it back to her to practice a few more times before you take it away for good. If she has something that could hurt her, like a pair of scissors or the string from a balloon, take it away and make sure she can't get to it again. For safe items, like your dirty shirt, let her take it again to practice *drop it* a few more times before you put it away, and promise yourself to do a better job of keeping the puppy's area clean.

10. If she does not drop the item easily, ask your parents for help. You'll need to practice this a lot so that she doesn't take things and run. If you chase her—even once—it will be harder.

10 Short But Challenging Stays

Since you want your puppy to *stay* no matter what you are doing, focus on distractions. Practice lots of short *stays* where you are close by and doing something that may distract your puppy. Ask your puppy to *stay* while you try the following challenges. Be sure to click and treat each time your puppy is successful!

1. Your puppy will *stay* while you bend over as if to tie your shoe and then stand up straight.
2. Your puppy will *stay* when someone else in your family opens the front door. (You are standing right beside your puppy, helping her make the right choice.)
3. Your puppy will *stay* while you take one step back and do one jumping jack.
4. Your puppy will *stay* when one of your siblings runs down the hallway.

5. Your puppy will *stay* when you turn your back and count to three.
6. Your puppy will *stay* when you walk two steps to the right and then two steps to the left.
7. Your puppy will *stay* when you wiggle your whole body for a count of 3.
8. Your puppy will *stay* if you move a book from the table to the sofa.
9. Your puppy will *stay* if you put the book on the floor 4 feet away from her. (Many puppies will want to go see whatever you put on the floor.)
10. Your puppy will *stay* if you have a very short conversation with another family member. Both of you must speak.

Once your puppy is really good at these short but distracting *stays*, you can start making them even more challenging by moving a little farther away or waiting a little longer before you click and treat.

Fun and Games

Your puppy is learning all the time, whether you think you are training her or not. Get creative. Look for ways to challenge your puppy, so that she'll grow up supersmart and be a great friend for you.

RULES

All games come with a few rules, and playing with your puppy is no exception. Good games are calm, gentle, and fair.

- **Calm.** Wild games are not a good idea. There should not be any screeching, yelling, or chasing. If your puppy gets revved up and starts jumping, it's time to stop for a while.
- **Gentle.** Don't push, pull, or hit your puppy. Roughhousing is not allowed. Similarly, if your puppy starts biting, call a time-out.
- **Fair.** A game is fun only when everyone wants to play. Either you or your puppy should be allowed to end a game at any time. No game should involve an activity that makes a player sad or uncomfortable. For example, most dogs do not enjoy playing dress-up!

TRICKS

There's nothing cuter than a puppy who does tricks. This section has a few basic ones you can try. If your puppy enjoys learning new tricks, look for a trick-training class or a good book on trick training, like *The Trick Is in the Training*, by Stephanie J. Taunton and Cheryl S. Smith. Your imagination is the only limit! Be creative and have fun.

Crawl

Before you can teach your puppy how to *crawl*, you need to teach her to *lie down*. Look in the training chapter for tips if your puppy doesn't know *down* yet.

Try It

1. Put five or six treats in one hand and your clicker in the other.
2. Lure your puppy into a *down* position. Give her one treat for lying down.
3. Now move your hand just a teeny bit farther away from her nose, and show her another treat. (The distance you move your hand depends on how big your puppy is. For a tiny puppy, you may move less than an inch. For a larger one, you may go as far as 2 inches (5 cm). Make it close enough so that it's not worth standing up, but far enough that she'll have to stretch to reach it.)
4. When your puppy moves toward the treat, click and give it to her.
5. Now move your hand again, just beyond her reach. Show her your next treat.
6. When your puppy moves toward the treat, click and give her a treat. Reward her for each "step."
7. At first you'll be able to move only very short distances between treats, but as your puppy figures out the game, she'll go farther and farther.

Having trouble?

• If your puppy is standing up to get the treat, you are probably moving it too far. Try shortening the distance.
• If your puppy stops moving forward, make sure you are rewarding her each time she goes forward. If you keep moving your hand away without giving her the treat, she'll feel like you are teasing her and will give up.

Spin

Most dogs are better at spinning in one direction than the other. Does your puppy have a favorite way to turn around?

Try It

1. Have three treats in one hand and your clicker in the other.
2. When your puppy is standing up, put your treat hand right in front of her nose and begin to slowly move your hand in a curved motion (as if you were going to draw a large circle around your puppy).
3. Your puppy should follow the treat. When you get one-third of the way around your imaginary circle, click and give her one treat.

4. Keep going for another third of the circle. Click and treat.
5. When you get back to the starting point, click and give her the last treat.
6. As she gets better, you can give her a treat for the first half and the second half. Eventually she'll go all the way around for only one treat at the end.

Having trouble?

• If your puppy sits down in the middle, you may be going too far before you reward— or she may be a bit large for your arm to reach far enough around her.
• If your puppy is jumping, make sure you hold the treat at nose level.

Roll Over

Your puppy must know *down* before she can learn to do this trick. Think of it as four pieces: lie down, lie on one side, lie on your back, and lie on the other side. You'll reward for each step.

Man's Best Friend

How did dogs become "man's best friend"? Why not geckos or koalas or leopards? There are millions of different animal species, and thousands of different mammals. What makes dogs so special?

The theory is that dogs first began living on the outskirts of villages about 15,000 years ago, scavenging food, eating garbage, and killing rodents. The dogs' ability to detect the presence of strangers or dangerous animals benefited the community as well. Over time, the friendliest dogs got better food and care from people, which allowed them to live longer. With each generation, dogs formed more connections with people.

Since dogs, like people, live in social groups and communicate with one another all the time, it was easy to learn to live with and love each other.

Try It

1. With your puppy lying down, hold a treat in front of her nose.
2. Slowly move your hand toward her side (aiming toward her shoulder).
3. As she turns to sniff the treat, she'll curve her spine and start rolling onto one side. Click and give her a treat.
4. Do this several times until she's comfortable with it.
5. When you are ready to try to get her to go farther, use a treat to keep luring her over. Your hand will actually be moving in a curve starting from her nose, going toward her shoulder, and finally heading toward the floor.
6. When your puppy rolls farther, click and give her a treat. This can be confusing for your puppy, so give her lots of treats for making progress. Soon she'll be able to roll all the way over every time.

Having trouble?

- This can be a bit harder for dogs with short legs and thick bodies. Take your time.

- If your puppy seems nervous about this trick, be sure to take things slowly. Don't push her over, because that will make her feel even more awkward and uncomfortable.

Take a Bow

When your puppy bows, she keeps her hind legs straight and bends her forelegs to the floor. You'll often see dogs bow when they play together.

Try It

1. Start with your puppy in a standing position and some treats in your hand. (It won't work if your puppy starts from a *sit*.)
2. Move your hand from her nose straight down to the floor. As she follows the treat with her nose, your puppy will start to hunch her body over your hand. Give her a treat or two as you lure her into position.
3. When your hand reaches the floor, slowly move your hand toward her body, just a little bit at a time. This will move her farther back on her elbows. Click and give her a treat when her elbows touch the ground.

Having trouble?

- If your puppy lies down, take the treat away and start over. Next time, you can try putting your other hand beneath her belly to remind her to keep her hips in the air.
- If your puppy paws at your hand, try to move more slowly and be sure to give her a few treats along the way to keep her feeling successful.

Touch Your Hand

Training your puppy to touch your hand is a good starting point for many other tricks.

Try It

1. Put your treats and clicker in one hand and keep your other hand empty.
2. Show your puppy your empty palm. Put your flat hand close to—but not touching—her nose.
3. When she leans forward and touches your palm with her nose, click and give her a treat from your other hand.
4. Take your target hand away and put it behind your back. Your hand should be there for only one or two seconds before you take it away (whether your puppy touches it or not).
5. Show your puppy your palm again. Put your hand in a slightly different spot each time, but always keep it close to her nose.
6. Once she's good at touching your palm anywhere it appears near her face, add a little distance. When she's standing, try putting your palm about 6 inches (15 cm) away. Will she move toward it to touch? If she does, click and treat.

Having trouble?

- If your puppy doesn't seem to understand what you want, make it easier. Put your palm very close to her face (within 2 inches [5 cm]). From there, it's easy for her to just stretch her neck to touch it. Also try this trick when your puppy is standing rather than sitting. Sometimes that helps her to be more active.
  - Don't leave your hand there too long. Give your puppy two seconds (count "one Mississippi, two Mississippi" in your head) before you take your hand away. Think of it like a game. She has two seconds to make a prizewinning choice or else, too bad, she has to wait for the next round.

Touch an Object

Once your puppy understands the Touch Game with your hand, she'll be ready to try it with an object. Let's try it with a large ball, like a soccer ball or basketball—something too big for her to put in her mouth.

1. Have your clicker in your hands and your treats nearby.
2. Just as you did with your flat palm, you'll put the ball about 2 inches (5 cm) away from your puppy's face.
3. When she leans forward and touches the ball with her nose, click and give her a treat.
4. Take the ball away and start over. Put it in a slightly different spot each time.
5. Once she's good at touching the ball when you hold it anywhere near her face, try putting it on the ground. Will she move toward it to touch? If she does, click and treat.

GOOFY GAMES

Which Hand?

This may be the simplest puppy game of all time, but it's always fun.

Try It

1. With a smelly treat in one fist and nothing in the other, put out both of your fists for your puppy to sniff.
2. Hold your hands still. Watch to see which fist she chooses. When she is sniffing one fist more than the other, open your hand.
3. If the treat is in that hand, let her eat it.
4. If the treat is not in that hand, put both of your hands behind your back. You can either switch the treat to the other hand or keep it where it is before you bring your fists out to give your puppy another chance.

Having trouble?

- Your puppy should get it right at least three tries out of every four. If she doesn't, try using a smellier treat. Your last chicken nugget, perhaps?

Hansel and Gretel Trails

Just as Hansel and Gretel laid a trail of bread crumbs to help them find their way home, you can create a trail for your puppy to follow on her own adventure.

Try It

1. Get a large handful of dog food or treats.
2. Either put your puppy in her crate or ask one of your parents to keep your puppy busy for a few minutes while you prepare the trail.
3. Picture the path that you want your puppy to follow. Put one piece of dog food every 6 to 8 inches (15–20 cm) along the path.

> ## Ice Bucket Yummies
> Get a medium-sized bowl, a food-stuffed chew toy, some loose kibble, and a few carrots or other vegetables. Put everything in the bowl. Fill it with water and freeze it for a delicious mental challenge in the backyard. She'll be like a puppy paleontologist excavating in search of dinosaur bones or other wonderful surprises.

4. When the trail is ready, let your puppy start at the beginning and work her way to the end.
5. As she gets better at this, you can start putting the pieces of dog food farther apart. You can also time her to see how long it takes for her to clean up the entire path.

Puppy Pop Quiz

**Q: Dogs are color-blind.
True or false?**

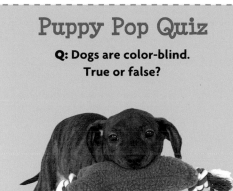

A: False. Dogs see colors, but not the same way we do. To a dog, the world is mostly yellow, blue, and gray. Colors like red and dark green usually seem black or brownish gray. If you want your puppy's toys to catch her eye, look for yellow or blue toys, not red ones.

Having trouble?

- If your puppy skips pieces of food, it may be that they are spaced too far apart and she's stopping to look around to find the next piece. Make sure she can see the next piece at each stopping point.

Homemade Obstacles

Build some simple obstacles for your puppy to try. Nothing scary! You never want your puppy to be frightened. Here are a few ideas to try for your own puppy playground:

- Put a broom across two kitchen chairs. Drape a towel over it. Will your puppy push through the towel to get to you?

Dogs with Jobs

Dogs' special skills can be used to help people with many different jobs.

- Assistance dogs help people with disabilities. These dogs help people with tasks they can't do alone, such as retrieving items, turning lights on and off, and helping with clothing.
- Detection dogs sniff out unwanted things, including drugs, chemicals, termites, snakes, and even cancer.
- Guard dogs patrol and protect property.
- Terriers are often used to seek out and get rid of rodents.
- Search-and-rescue dogs help find lost people. They can follow a trail when someone is lost in the woods or help find victims of disasters, such as earthquakes or hurricanes.
- Military dogs have been scouts, messengers, and even mine detectors.
- Herding dogs can move groups of sheep on ranches, but they're also used at airports to keep runways clear of geese and other birds that could interfere with the planes taking off and landing.
- Therapy dogs bring joy to people in hospitals and nursing homes.

- Put a thick marker underneath a scrap of plywood, making it a very low teeter-totter. See if your puppy will walk over it.
- Get a large box and open both ends to make a tunnel. Can your puppy walk through it?

- Line up three or four empty 2-liter bottles. Can you use treats to help your puppy weave through them?
- Use the same 2-liter bottles and play "puppy bowling." Set them up as a barrier between you and your puppy. Then call her to see if she'll crash through the bottle blockade.

Cooling System

Dogs have an amazing cooling system. Because they have sweat glands only between their paw pads, they need another way to cool off, so they use a special form of heavy breathing called panting. When the dog inhales, the air passes over the moist tissues of the mouth and nose. Evaporation helps the dog's body cool down.

When the dog exhales, the outgoing air is about 10 degrees hotter than the incoming air. This system is interesting, but it is not as efficient as your body's way of cooling off. Be careful not to let your puppy overheat.

- Build a fort with the couch cushions. Crawl inside and call your puppy. Will she come in too? (Make sure the fort won't fall down on her!)
- Lay a hula-hoop on the floor. Can you get your puppy to sit inside it?
- Hold the hula-hoop upright. Can you get your puppy to walk through it?

Remember to click and treat whenever your puppy succeeds. Make it fun for your puppy!

Puppy Pop Quiz

Q: Dogs can hear things people can't. True or false?

A: True. At lower levels, people and dogs have similar abilities, but dogs can hear more high-pitched noises better. They also can identify many quieter sounds that we miss. Your puppy may be able to identify the sound of your car from the top of the street. She will know you are home before you even get out of the car.

Beat the Clock

This game teaches your puppy to respond quickly when you give her a cue. Once your puppy knows the cue word for several different skills, you two will be ready for this fun game. Be careful not to let your puppy get too excited!

Try It

1. Have your treat bag on and your clicker in your hand.
2. Starting from right beside your puppy, rush to a spot about 4 feet (1.2 m) away. Ask her to *sit*.
3. When she sits, click and toss a treat for her to find on the floor.
4. Then rush to a different spot.
5. After she eats the treat and comes toward you, ask her to *lie down*.
6. When she does, you'll click, toss a treat for her to find, and rush away again.
7. If she makes a mistake, stop and help her get it right.
8. Try this with all the words she knows. The real fun for your puppy is wondering where you'll go and what you'll ask for next!

Having trouble?

- This is an advanced game. Make sure your puppy knows the words, not just the physical cues, for each behavior.

DOG SPORTS

When your puppy gets a bit older and has completed a basic obedience class, she might enjoy trying one of the popular dog sports. Just as some kids like gymnastics and others prefer the chess club, your puppy may show a strong preference for one kind of activity over another. Find an activity that is fun for both of you.

- **Agility.** Your puppy will learn to go over, around, and through obstacles like ramps, weave poles, and tunnels. As she gets better, it will become a timed race to see how quickly she can complete an entire course.

- **Flyball.** For dogs who love running for tennis balls, this sport is a hit. Your puppy will learn to jump over hurdles on her way to a spring-loaded box that contains a tennis ball. After she releases

94

the ball, she'll bring it back to you, jumping over the hurdles all the way. This is a relay race. Typically four dogs form a team, and their combined time is compared against other teams'. It's *fast*. Many teams can finish in less than 15 seconds!

- **Freestyle.** In this sport, you'll develop a routine (set to music) that combines obedience skills and tricks. Your puppy may weave between your legs, jump over your arm, spin in circles, or even walk on her hind legs, all as part of your dance.

- **Nosework.** Challenge your puppy to use her talented nose to seek and locate hidden scents. It's fascinating to watch your puppy work. You'll learn a lot about how she sees (or rather, smells) the world.

- **Rally Obedience.** If your puppy did well in a basic obedience class, she may really enjoy rally, which takes the skills you've already learned as well as a few more challenging ones and combines them to form a course. You'll move from place to place doing different skills. Scoring is based on how well your puppy performs each behavior.

- **Treibball.** If you don't happen to have a flock of sheep in your backyard, your puppy may think herding a giant ball is the next best thing. Since people can't touch the ball, you'll use lots of training to encourage your puppy to get the ball to the goal.

- **Tricks Classes.** Although not technically a dog sport, trick training is always a great activity for kids who like to be involved with their dogs. Many dog-training schools offer trick-training classes.

Conclusion

By now you've learned that the way you care for, train, and interact with your puppy can have a huge effect on how she will behave as an adult. She needs you and your family to help her grow up confident and well mannered.

It takes a lot of time and energy to properly socialize and train a puppy. It's not a job you can do in a few hours or a few days. Your puppy will need a lifetime of daily attention and support, and she'll repay you with lots of love and companionship. The two of you will have years of fun together!